I

Gary Hocking - the forg
Page 4 (
"the lat
At the time of publication Mr Costa
publisher apologise for any
Veloc

'SOX'

Gary Hocking
– the forgotten
World Motorcycle
Champion

Roger Hughes

www.veloce.co.uk

For post publication news, updates and amendments relating to this book please visit www.veloce.co.uk/books/V4862

First published in April 2016 by Veloce Publishing Limited, Veloce House, Parkway Farm Business Park, Middle Farm Way, Poundbury, Dorchester DT1 3AR, England. Fax 01305 268864 / e-mail info@veloce.co.uk / web www.veloce.co.uk or www.velocebooks.com.
ISBN: 978-1-845848-62-0. UPC: 6-36847-04862-4

Main cover picture: Gary Hocking (MV Agusta), 1961 Junior TT – Courtesy Mortons Archive.

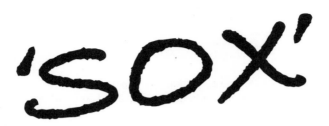

'SOX'

Gary Hocking – the forgotten World Motorcycle Champion

Roger Hughes

VELOCE PUBLISHING
THE PUBLISHER OF FINE AUTOMOTIVE BOOKS

Acknowledgements

I would like to thank the following, without whose help this book would not have been possible. I list them in no particular order, and I am certain I have missed someone out, in which case I apologise:

Jim Redman, for his memories of motorcycle racing at the time and his recollections of Gary Hocking; Nobby Clark, for his reflections of time spent with Sox; Bob Dowty and the late George Costain, for their memories of the young rider who came to learn the TT course; Shaun and Tommy Robinson, for their recollections of life in Rhodesia; Bobby Dixon, for his contribution to Gary's early racing career; John Surtees and Phil Read, for memories of racing against Gary Hocking; Dave 'Squak' Harris, whom I constantly bombarded with questions and requests for information; Marius Matthee, who provided race reports at a time when the project looked to be stalling; Stephen Jackson at the Manx Museum, for the hours he spent searching for newspaper articles; John Watterson, for supplying photographs, proofreading some of the chapters, and general enthusiasm for the project; Belfast Libraries, for information on the Ulster Grand Prix; Pretoria State Library and *The Bulawayo Chronicle*, for searches; Tim Parnell, for his memories of Gary in the Lotus; Tony Cleverley, for his recollections of Gary the driver; Grahams Motorcycles (Taunton), for its help identifying the MZs; Rennie Mackrory, for his eyewitness account of the fatal accident; Bill Snelling of FoTTofinders, Billy James, Morag Tritt, and Caroline Foden Williams, for providing photographs; Peter and Sue Corrin for accommodation on the Isle of Man; Val Church, for her memories of life and love with Gary; John Wells, who has been an encouragement from the outset, and despite trials and tribulations has proofread chapters, spent hours recalling times with Gary and searching out photographs.

Finally to Duncan Hocking, who answered the three questions: are you Gary's brother, have you an attic full of memorabilia, and will you help? (And said yes to all three.) I hope this book does your brother credit and keeps the name alive.

Roger Hughes

Contents

Foreword by Don Morley

THE WORLD WAS a very different place when the paths of quietly spoken and deeply religious Gary Hocking and I crossed. We were both staying at the same boarding house, as it happened, for the 1958 TT. This was an era when motorcycle racing, wherever it took place, was very much more dangerous than today, and when very few race organisers or circuit owners bothered much about rider safety.

Sand traps and safety run-offs remained as yet unheard of. Indeed, even adding a few extra, strategically placed straw bales was regarded as a needless luxury. Everyone in racing simply accepted the fact that the riders, and most especially the seemingly never-ending stream of new young Commonwealth riders, would be regarded almost as cannon fodder.

Many riders had been and would be killed, including Gary Hocking's own great southern Rhodesian predecessor, Ray Amm, but such was the enthusiasm for our sport that most riders just accepted the danger on the basis of "Okay, it happens, but not to me." So it was with 21-year-old Gary, who, like so many other Commonwealth riders, had learned his track skills on the mostly grass or dirt circuits back home in Bulawayo.

In those days, the motorcycle racing world was very different off track, too. Hence, Gary, like most other Commonwealth riders who came over to Europe to try their luck, always, when out and about, very proudly wore his home country's uniform: green blazer with embroidered national federation breast pocket badge, flannels, and, of course, rather like today's rugby players, the regulation FIM tie.

Anyway, although like ships that passed in the night, Gary and I somehow became great friends that 1958 TT week. I discovered that he had chanced coming over to Europe on a wing and a prayer, with his racing leathers, but without any actual machinery to race. Beyond that, all he had was the clothes he was wearing, plus his life savings of £200. Luckily, he knew Jim Redman, who put in a good word for him with Reg Dearden, who was that era's greatest UK sponsor.

Dearden thus agreed to lend Gary a secondhand 500cc Manx Norton, and the rest, of course, is history, as covered so well within this book. Gary might have been the quiet man of motorcycle racing, but he certainly seized his chances with both hands: that same season he finished sixth at the Dutch TT (on his by-then well and truly outclassed Norton), fourth at the Swedish, and, even more incredibly, third at the German GP where, outclassed or not, he beat all of the factory-entered BMWs, *and* split the two works 500cc MVs.

Unsurprisingly, this latter feat earned him a brace of better Nortons, plus the offer of a factory lightweight ride with the East German MZ team, for whom Gary then won the Ulster and Swedish Grands Prix, not only beating Mike Hailwood whilst at it, but also thrashing reigning multi-world champion Carlo Ubbiali and his MV Agustas – achievements that brought him an MV factory contract to ride all classes as required. This, I rather suspect, was initially so as to make sure he rode to orders, and thus did not keep beating the great Carlo Ubbiali.

Gary and I kept in regular touch and enjoyed many long and often deep conversations between races. However, increasingly it seemed that Gary, even as a multiple world champion, had become deeply troubled about his future within the sport. I knew, although he hardly ever mentioned it, that without fail Gary went to church to seek solace every Sunday that was not a race day.

He also worried that it had all been a bit too easy for him. He wondered why he had been able to come over to Europe and easily beat so many of his own heroes, and he felt there was something not quite right about that. Although he gave no quarter once on a bike, and was never less than 100 per cent competitive, he also worried increasingly about so many other riders being killed.

Gary, quite literally, prayed his own competitiveness would never, ever, be even partly to blame for someone else's death. To him this concern was very obviously becoming an ever greater burden. We had a lengthy – but very matter-of-fact, and in no way morbid – discussion about this on the eve of the 1962 Junior (350cc) TT world championship, when Gary made a statement which, to use the modern idiom, quite literally blew me away.

We were standing by the TT circuit on the Sunday evening before race week, watching the antics of the fans overcooking it, when Gary said he knew that if he carried on racing he was going to get killed. He added "I'm already a world champion and I have had been made an MBE, what else do I need to prove?" This was obviously a well considered but completely out of the blue statement, which, to this day, remains emblazoned on my own mind.

Gary went on to explain that he still wanted to enjoy the thrill of racing, so he was going to switch to racing cars on the basis that he would then have a bit more protection round him, and thus would be at least a tad safer!

This, incidentally, was being said to a friend who was still a press photographer and occasional journalist, and who could truly have capitalised on what was looking then like THE story of a lifetime, had I blabbed it.

The following day a great tragedy struck when Tom Phillis, who was Gary's and my friend, was killed at Laurel Bank during the Junior, whilst trying too hard to catch Gary who, despite any personal worries, was, as usual, the race's leader.

Many others have suggested that Gary decided to retire from motorcycle racing directly because of Tom's death, but I know different. However, it was a measure of the man that he gave no quarter to anyone when racing, despite his personal demons. He not only won that ill-fated Junior TT race, but carried on to win the following Friday's Senior.

However, these successes brought problems. The MV team had agreed to travel immediately after the TT to Mallory Park, in Leicestershire, to compete in the International Post-TT race, which in those days was a quite massive big money event. It was the only event at which the English home fans got to see the world championship contending Grand Prix riders and their exotic machines.

Gary was contracted to go to Mallory Park. However, he told my wife, Jo, and I that he did not want to go, and would rather just stop racing motorcycles then and there, but, typical Gary, he was also wrestling with his conscience and did not want to let the expectant fans down (he had not yet announced his retirement). After much discussion, and soul searching, he decided to honour his contract and go to Mallory to race, despite his personal misgivings.

As ever, this oh-so-honourable gentleman won that race in great style and by the proverbial mile. A great feat when no-one other than my wife and I, and by then the MV mechanics, had any idea this was to be his last race, as he planned to go to the MV factory on the Monday to hand the bikes back to Count Agusta and tell him in person why he could not continue, and also offer to buy himself out of his MV contract. The Count understood, and waived Gary's contract without deducting his pay.

After the discussions I have described and having photographed his Mallory win, that was it – Gary and I never spoke or saw each other again. Then came the awful and truly ironic news that he had indeed been killed racing, but rather than whilst racing a motorbike, dear Gary had somehow met his end on his first time out in a racing car.

The crash that killed him was on 21st December 1962, and happened between corners, and to this day has never been explained. Gary was having his first ever test in a F1 racing car, which he was hoping to race in that season's non-championship counting South African GP, being held in Durban.

I could never understand why such a lovely, God-fearing man had been recalled by his maker in such a tragic manner.

On a personal front, Gary will always live on, not least as my wife Jo was already carrying our eldest son when we heard the news, so we decided, then and there, to christen him 'Gary' after our wonderful friend. Not only was Gary the most genuinely nice person I ever knew, but someone who always challenged – and so often beat – the best in our sport, including the likes of Mike Hailwood. Had he carried on racing motorcycles rather than switching to cars, Gary might well have won many more two-wheeler world titles, and might also still be with us.

RIP Gary.

Don Morley

1

The early years

A TEENAGER WENT to his headmaster and asked, "Sir, I want to become a motorcyclist, and I think I might make world class. Shall I go with it, or shall I stay in Bulawayo and become a draughtsman?"

Gary Hocking was that teenager, he made his choice, and he became world class. At the age of 25, just a few short years after posing that question to his headmaster at Bulawayo Technical College, his affair with speed was over.

It was whilst looking for the grave of my grandparents that I came across a simple, grey, slightly weathered gravestone, which initially looked no different to any of the other stones that mark the last resting places of people buried in Christchurch cemetery, Newport, South Wales. Maybe because it was near the end of a row, maybe after all there was something different about it, or maybe there was something in the engraving which attracted my attention. It read "Gary Hocking MBE, Double World Motorcycle Champion."

I had never heard of Gary Hocking, but having an interest in all sport, and obviously needing to fill a gap in my knowledge of a successful sporting Welshman, I needed to find out more about someone who, if the inscription was correct, had made his mark in motorcycle history.

Returning the short distance home, I immediately cranked up the computer and searched the name 'Gary Hocking.' I'm not sure what I expected. Maybe some over-enthusiastic parent had called a minor motorcycle event a world championship, maybe our mystery man had ridden a Vespa scooter, or a mowing machine fitted with a motorbike engine of limited capacity! Even back in the early '60s, anything seemed to qualify for the title 'world championship.'

It was almost as if I was hoping to prove my theory correct, and the inscription on the gravestone a fraud, when the page on my subject came up. As I read the information, I could feel my jaw drop as the list of achievements unfolded – the riders Hocking had ridden against, and beaten. I had heard of the names

Hailwood, Duke, Minter, and Surtees, and knew that in the world of the motorbike, they were the big players of their day.

Having been several times to the Isle of Man TT races, I knew that to win one of those was indeed a major accomplishment, and to become a world champion at 350cc and 500cc was rather far from a Vespa scooter or a machine rigged up from parts in a backstreet garage. As I read on I can remember literally uttering an audible 'Wow!' The story that unfolded was fascinating, it was exciting, and in the end it was sad.

I felt I had to make the short walk back to the cemetery, if only to apologise to the occupant of the grave that I had ever doubted the credibility of the owner, and to just feel close to someone who had already grabbed my attention, and my interest, and someone I just had to know more about.

Sitting on a bench in Newport's Christchurch cemetery, it's relaxing to look across to Twm Barlam and its pimple. In the valley below, the river Usk meanders its way to the Bristol Channel, the tide ebbing and flowing on its twice-daily sequence. In the distance stands the Sugar Loaf mountain and Cordell Country, rough and rugged, but with its own particular beauty. The town of Caerleon sits on the river bank, once a home to the Roman army which named it Isca.

The peace is eroded by the constant drone of the traffic on the M4 motorway, but back in January 1963 when Gary Hocking was buried, there was no motorway traffic struggling up the hill before falling down towards the infamous Brynglas tunnels and on to Cardiff. The only sound then would have been the birds, the sounds of the traffic on the road below making its way between Newport and Caerleon, and possibly the odd train chugging its way towards Pontypool and the Eastern valley.

It can be a cold place on the side of the hill, with the north wind blowing down the Usk Valley, and as I read the inscription on the gravestone for the umpteenth time, it dawned on me that Hocking's remains had laid there for over 50 years. There had to be more to discover about someone who had achieved greatness in his sport, and been honoured by the Queen in the process.

A trip to the local library was disconcerting, and also amazing. Apart from an obituary there was little about one of the local sporting heroes. Much had changed in those fifty-odd years, and time had obviously forgotten someone who should have been remembered and recognised by the current generation. More investigation was to discover that Gary Hocking had a brother, and he would probably hold the key to unlocking this story further. Finding him would be the first objective.

There were three references to Hocking in the local library. One was a piece that carried the headline "Hocking lands contract with Cooper." The article, scripted by George Scrivens in the *South Wales Argus*, continued: "Newport-born speed ace Gary Hocking will drive an eight-cylinder Cooper Climax in the South African Grand Prix at Port Elizabeth on December 27th."

The second reference, in the same newspaper three days later, dated December 21st 1962, reported the death of Gary Hocking. "Newport racing driver dies in practice crash," was the headline. The article went on to describe how the 25-year-old had died from injuries received when his car left the track during the practice session for the Natal Grand Prix.

The third reference didn't relate to Gary at all, but to another Hocking: Duncan. We knew from internet research that Gary had a brother, but that research also led us to believe that he lived in America. If that was still the case the story was probably a non-starter, as to carry out in-depth research from that sort of distance would be difficult. However, a posting on a message board suggested that the brother had moved back to South Wales.

Now, South Wales stretches from Fishguard in the west to Chepstow in the east, and there could be a fair few Hockings living in that geographical area. The hope was that family roots in Newport, or at least east Wales, might have proved an attraction if Duncan had returned to the UK. The telephone directory showed a Hocking in Cardiff, although not with the initial 'D,' so the call was made. Well, whoever answered the phone recited poetry and sang songs down the line, so even if this was the brother, he was going to be of little use to us in recalling the life of someone who died 50 years ago. Another number threw up an address in Newport, where the person told us that he had had this enquiry before, but sorry, wasn't related.

Then the third *South Wales Argus* article surfaced, headlined "Just Seconds from Disaster." Leanne Fender wrote, "Two Gwent drag racers are lucky to be alive after their transporter vehicle exploded ... Alan Terry from Cwmbran and Duncan Hocking from Pontypool."

The problem here was that the article was written in September 2008, and there was no Hocking listed in Pontypool. Friends came up with several suggestions, such as getting help from the local motorcycle community. This drew a blank. The best hope was the electoral roll, in Pontypool library. Unfortunately, the electoral roll isn't in alphabetical order, but after trawling through page after page I can safely say that there is only one Hocking family living in Pontypool electoral area.

Armed with the address, I turned up with three hopes at the forefront of my mind. One, that it was the right Duncan Hocking; two, that he had an attic full of pictures, articles, and memorabilia; and three, that he was happy to help with the research. After a nervous wait at the door, the answers came – yes I am, yes I have, and yes I will.

It was interesting at this point to discover that Duncan called his brother Gaerey, rather than Gary with a hard 'r.' Apparently, his mother preferred the former, softer, version of the name, and so the elder Hocking was always called Gaerey within his family.

Gary and his younger brother, Duncan, lived with their parents, Arthur and Marjory, at number 10 Llanwern Road in Newport. At that time in the 1940s this was part of the Caerleon area. Now, with Newport having achieved city status and, like so many urban areas, pushed its boundaries into the fields and former countryside, Llanwern Road is well and truly part of the conurbation.

Llanwern Road was the gateway to the farms and open spaces; a place to play, and a place to run free. There was a seven-year gap between the two boys, and in some ways Duncan feels he missed a closer relationship. "He was always there, he must have been, but with him being ten when I was three I don't think we played much together, "said Duncan.

This part of Newport has changed greatly over the 60 years since the Hockings lived at number ten. Now, rather than leading to farms, fields and the countryside, Llanwern Road leads to one of the large housing estates built to cope with slum clearance and Newport's increasing population in the 1950s. Dwellings have been built on both sides of the road, and the houses have even been renumbered, so that number ten is now number nine. It's a far cry from the environment enjoyed in the 1940s.

Gary went to a primary school up the hill at Christchurch, but as pupil numbers fell that disappeared. The site is now occupied by a car park and viewing point, giving uninterrupted views right up the Usk valley on a clear day.

Marshall Butler was a schoolmate of Hocking's, and he recalls the school as being a red brick building typical of its time, though there are some similar buildings still around today. There were juniors and seniors, taught by seven teachers. Butler recalls: "They were all spinsters – Miss Walker Drew, Bryant, and Page. There was also Mr Owens and Mr Harper, and the headmaster was Mr Hancock. There were a lot of evacuees from London, and they were rough kids. I recall one of them running along the top of the dining table with food going everywhere and being chased by the headmaster with his stick." On the days when Gary returned home with a black eye or bloody nose as a result of fighting on the mile or so journey down the hill back to home, it may have been one of the evacuees responsible. Duncan can't recall whether his brother would have been the aggressor or the bullied in such circumstances, but even in a country area like Christchurch, boys would be boys.

Barton recalls that he liked Gary, who he thought was clever and very good at drawing. "One day he asked me if I wanted to come and see a coconut, I hadn't got as clue what a coconut was," said Barton, "but we went to his house and he showed me what I think his uncle had brought back from his travels in the army. We drank the contents."

The Hocking home, Duncan recalls, was a comfortable and happy one. The boys' father, Arthur, was a metal turner in one of Newport's factories, whilst their mother was a bookkeeper and accounts manager in Moorwells, a Cardiff motor franchise. The family was well-off compared with many who had suffered during the war. The Hockings weren't a particularly sporting family, although his uncle, his mother's brother, did play water polo for Wales in the early 1930s.

Arthur was the youngest of a big family, which Duncan believes may have given him a tendency to become slightly withdrawn. "My father wasn't big on family. Having been brought up in a big family he probably wanted to get out of it, get on his own and be left alone, so he led a rather solitary existence. Except, if he was amongst a group of friends there would be moments when he would be the life and soul of the party. He would be the one performing tricks, doing this and doing that, then at home he would be very quiet; probably something to do with his upbringing. No one has ever said anything to me, I have only thought about that myself, and thought perhaps that was the reason he was the way he was. He wasn't big on family unfortunately, got along with my mother well, didn't get along with my brother, but got along with me okay, but I was the quiet one, I just sort of fitted in."

Motorbikes had an early part to play in the life of Arthur and Marjory Hocking, or to give her correct first name, Ira. On their first date Arthur turned up on a motorbike. "I never intended going out with him again," Marjory told Duncan much later, but apparently Arthur had a crash and broke either his arm or his leg, Duncan couldn't remember. Marjory found herself visiting Arthur in hospital, and that is how the relationship began.

Motorbikes were eventually to play an important part in the life of the Hocking family, with both Gary and Duncan achieving success in their respective disciplines.

Life in 1947, just two years after the end of the Second World War, was depressed and depressing. Rationing was still uppermost in people's minds as the country tried to recover from the shortages. Transport was limited, and luxuries were few and far between, even if a family could afford them.

No housewife went shopping without her ration book, and even with the right coupons, food was in such short supply that basic commodities were not always available. If you could get them, cigarettes such as Park Drive, Woodbines, or Players Weights, some of the popular choices of the day, were around a shilling (five pence) for 20. A pint of beer was ten old pence to a shilling, a loaf of bread four old pence (less than two and half-pence in today's money), chips one penny, fish three, and a gallon of petrol – if you were wealthy enough to own a car – was ten pence a gallon. To own a small car in those days would see the purchaser part with something in the region of £700.

Later in the year, the weekly ration of meat from the butcher had been chopped to one shilling's worth, by law petrol was available only for essential motoring not for pleasure, and holidaying abroad was banned. Worse still, potatoes were on the restricted list for the first time. It was also a Britain of smog in the cities and chilblains for children clustering round coal fires. No central heating, but fewer allergies.

At the start of 1947 even the weather did its best to heap misery on the population. If people weren't fed up enough with their lot, it was one of the worst winters ever experienced. In late February heavy snow fell across Monmouthshire, and in March Newport experienced the heaviest snow fall in its history. Around the outskirts of the town there were 20- to 30-foot snow drifts. Supplies of essentials couldn't be delivered.

Freezing winds brought everything to a halt. Road transport was crippled, as were railways, which also affected the movement of coal, which was needed to keep the houses warm and fire the power stations. Consequently as stocks became low so power cuts were the order of the day. Even the river Usk which flows through the town had a film of ice from bank to bank.

It all went to make Britain a miserable place, and life in those times was hard. People had suffered the war years, now they were suffering in the peace as well. The government adopted emergency powers over a country that felt itself not at peace but under siege. The Prime Minister, Clement Attlee, was gloomy: "I have no easy words for the nation. I cannot say when we will emerge into easier times."

In some ways though, the weather apart, this was a Britain to yearn for. A Britain of corner shops and not supermarkets, leaf tea not teabags, quaint Austin Sevens and Ford Eights not SUVs and BMWs, red telephone boxes not iPhones, of words in full not initials, of grammar not text-speak.

It was a Britain to which prosperity would return, and life in general was coming back to normal, albeit slowly. The local football club, Newport County, was in the old second division, although would finish the '46-'47 season relegated, but the following season would spend a transfer record fee of £5000 signing Bryn Allen from Cardiff City.

Ken Jones was starting out on a rugby career with Newport which would see him gain 44 Welsh caps, a record for its time, and also make a name for himself as a sprinter, with the lure of the London 1948 Olympics on the horizon.

The Newport Athletic Club, of which the rugby section was a major part, was picking up the pieces after the war. Athletics, tennis, hockey bowls, badminton, table tennis, bridge, netball and cricket offered recreation for Newport people in 1947. If playing wasn't their option, then watching enabled cricket followers to see the skills of the likes of Walter Hammond, Dennis Compton, and Len Hutton, who would have played against Glamorgan on the cricket ground at Rodney parade. Athletics meetings attracted the likes of Derek Ibbotson and Emmanuel McDonald Bailey.

It was this tired nation that summoned up all its energy to celebrate a royal wedding when Princess Elizabeth married Lieutenant Philip Mountbatten, in Westminster Abbey, the first major pageantry since the end of the war.

Legislation also moved on in Newport. In 1947, a referendum took place on Sunday cinema opening. Against the personal convictions of councillors in the town, 13,250 voted for cinemas to be open, 7862 against. A bylaw was repealed which would allow games to be played in the towns parks on a Sunday, but the doors of the pubs remained firmly shut on the Sabbath.

More importantly for our story, legislation came into force to alter some of the boundaries to coincide with the Newport borough boundaries. Areas of Maesglas, Gaer, Malpas and importantly Christchurch would vote with Newport, not Monmouthshire. Llanwern Road where the Hockings lived had been in Christchurch, Monmouthshire, not Newport, and Christchurch was part of Caerleon, which is why Gary Hocking's birth place is recorded as Caerleon, and not Newport.

In May 1947, major changes came about in Britain and in Wales. Railways were nationalised, as were the coal mines. More locally the Steel Company of Wales was formed of which the Newport firm of Lysaghts was a major part.

Like so many companies around the country, Lysaghts was more than just a work place; it was a community. A brass band, cricket team, football and rugby teams, and the institute where social gatherings could take place and where what was known as improvement courses were all provided for the huge workforce.

The Newport of 1947 was also home to a family by the name of Hope. Ivor, James and Emily were all born in the borough. The most famous member of the family though, Bob, who would be one of the big names in entertainment in later years, was born in London after the family had moved away.

Talking of entertainment, radios were becoming more popular and more widely used. Brown Bakelite or wooden models produced by companies such as Ekco, Bush, or Marconi would be tuned into the ever growing number of radio stations churning out the music of the day from singers such as Al Jolson, Frankie Lane, Perry Como, or the up and coming Frank Sinatra. Television hadn't reached the masses, and certainly hadn't reached outposts such as Newport.

From some quarters, predictably perhaps, came revolutionary warnings. There was a fear after the Second World War that communism was the big threat, and, as Churchill later called it, 'the Cold War' replaced the battlefield. Life in 1947 may have been utterly threadbare and unrecognisable compared with the Britain of today. It would be no surprise that people such as the Hockings decided that there was a better future to be had in the countries that went to make up the commonwealth. Rhodesia was one of those, awaiting skilled people with open arms. It was a country which in the 1930s had been made rich by its copper industry.

Duncan can remember little of Llanwern Road, or of the journey to Africa. He admits that, as a three-year old, he had little comprehension of the move. "Family life was very different in those days. We hadn't been outside Newport by then. There was very little money to do much anyway, and that was the reason we left. The opportunities weren't there, the country was strapped after the war. I do know that is why we went, but it is only because I asked later. At the time as a three-year old you just did what the family did, you didn't ask 'Why are we going to Africa dad?'"

Needless to say, for seven years older Gary, the whole exercise of packing, travelling, and the distance involved was probably more exciting, but for Duncan it's a memory lost in time. "Apart from the boat, the swimming pool on board, and the vastness of the ocean, I can't remember anything. I saw little of him, [Gary] though. He always seemed to be off adventuring somewhere, even on a ship in the middle of the ocean he found things to do."

Talking to Duncan now, you get the feeling that he regrets his lack of contact with his older brother. Little did he know then of course how little time he would have with Gary, but, as he says, "Ten-year olds don't tend to have much to do with three-year olds, unless there is a purpose to it. So I didn't really have a great deal of input with him."

Things were very different for the Hockings when they arrived in Bulawayo. A few years later, someone who would become a close friend of Gary Hocking, Jim Redman, would make the same journey from England to Rhodesia. Redman put his arrival in his own words, "It was called the jewel of Africa and it was. It was a beautiful country, well run, it was a happy place, the population was fantastic, black and white, and a lot of English people had emigrated there and it was a fantastic climate. There were plenty of jobs, I arrived as a mechanic and every garage I called at said I want you. I was really sad about leaving England, but when I got to Rhodesia I thought I had died and gone to heaven, the sun was shining and everyone was happy."

Duncan also experienced a new world, "The weather was different, and there were all these black people going around. We had a black servant helping us around the house, that was normal everyone did, but it wasn't the same as being in England, it was very different."

The Hockings brought a house and two acres of land five miles outside Bulawayo, which at that time was out in the bush. "I was told to be careful," recalls Duncan. His mother reinforced her warnings by telling her sons that there were snakes in the bush which would chase them!

Whilst Gary was at school and his parents working, Duncan would either be at home or in the Bulawayo municipal swimming pool, which attracted children all year round, or 'hunting' in the bush. Later Gary would be off on two wheels, firstly a push bike, but as early as 14 or 15 Duncan recalls Gary had got involved in motorbikes. "We lived in a different type of society there. You don't have the same sort of controls by the police" said Duncan. "In those days out there it wasn't that unusual to see a 14 or 15-year old on a motorcycle on the streets."

Gary obviously enjoyed life in his adopted country, and took advantage of the climate and the local amenities. He could often be found at the local swimming baths, where he would show early signs of his competitive spirit. He became well known for his athleticism, especially as a swimmer and diver, and had a tremendous lung capacity. He often challenged others to stay submerged for long periods, and always won.

Gary's first involvement with bikes was purely functional according to Duncan.

"We lived five or six miles out of town; he couldn't afford a car, so he saved up and got the bike."

Former school pal Derek Clark has further insight into Gary Hocking's first association with bikes. "We left school together and served apprenticeships with the Rhodesian Railways. Just before he started on the railways he brought a Jawa, and he used to ride that around." A powerful two-stroke motorcycle, the Jawa 250/350cc with the compact engine, rear wheel suspension and many other innovations, was exported to more than 120 countries worldwide. It was one of the make's most successful models.

"I remember the day we were due to start our apprenticeships he fell off the Jawa in the rain and caught pneumonia, so he didn't start his apprenticeship for another month. There wasn't much traffic about, and all of us thought that we were demons," added Clark.

Hocking and Clark first met up at Bulawayo Technical High School (locally known as 'tech') in 1951. "It was a technical school," recalls Clark, who like all Clarks is better known as 'Nobby.' "It only taught technical subjects such as mechanical engineering, carpentry, electronics, and that sort of stuff. In Rhodesia at the time we had academic schools and technical schools, and if you wanted to be a doctor, dentist or a lawyer you went to the academic school; if you wanted to be in the trades you went to the technical school." Hocking was a good pupil and was a favourite of his teacher, Mr Keith Pinchen, who would talk about Gary right up to the former's death in the early part of the millennium. Pinchen, who thought so highly of Gary, told people that he was clever practically and at the theory, and was a top student. He was very proud of Gary and what he had achieved. Hocking did his work and passed his exams at the end of his course, before going into the railways as a draughtsman.

It was also at school where Hocking was given his nickname 'Sox,' only because he disliked wearing them, and was constantly to be seen in what we would now call a pair of flip flops. Talking to people who knew Gary Hocking, they refer to him as Sox, more than Gary, or Hocking.

Another acquaintance was renewed with former school friend Marshall Butler, whose family had also emigrated to Rhodesia. Although Marshall had attended the Grammar school he wanted to become an engineer, and began an apprenticeship on the railways at the same time as Gary Hocking. "We worked on the general bench," said Butler. "We were grinding ball joints for steam pipes." They both hated the work, with Butler wanting to go to sea and Hocking wanting to use his drawing skills to become a draughtsman, but apparently they had fun, although the Rhodesians had little or no sense of humour.

Nobby Clark supports the feeling that Rhodesia was a good place to be in the early '50s. "We lived about three or four miles out of town and there weren't many people about. Gary, I think, lived further out, but even so it was open country, the houses weren't built on top of each other. We had a few sacrifices: just after the war petrol was rationed, a few food things were rationed – I can remember one of them being butter – but it wasn't that bad. I enjoyed life, I feel we grew up in a good environment."

Like all places, though, that was to change. In a letter Sox wrote to his mother at the end of October 1956, from 114 Rhodes Street, Bulawayo, after the rest of the family had returned to Wales, he said: "About a week ago a European, I think a Greek, was chopped up with an axe by some Kaffirs [the term used for black South Africans] because he had a Kaffir girlfriend. Also two white people were stoned in their car and were both killed." Hocking commented: "This place is turning into a real hoodlum joint!"

Nobby at this time was the one who was interested in motorbikes. Gary was more interested in music, and was often to be found playing his piano accordion or his mouth organ. Clark takes up the story again: "We had a milkshake bar down in the town. Gary played on a Friday night at the Coconut Bar. He would quite often win competitions there on the mouth organ or the piano accordion."

It was the money from the musical competition winnings along with occasional odd jobs around the town that financed Hocking's Jawa, which, according to Clark, wouldn't have cost a fortune. Before the Jawa came onto the scene Gary Hocking didn't have any interest in motorbikes; in fact, some say he disliked them. As a result of his rides to work, though, he caught the bug. He enjoyed throwing the machine about, the freedom, and the speed. He also showed his ability as a mechanic, he stripped the machine down and re-built it.

The comfortable family environment of the Hocking household was gradually to be shattered, though, when Arthur began to drink too heavily. It led to arguments between Arthur and Marjorie, which affected Gary more than Duncan. Duncan recalls a not particularly happy period in his family life. "They were careful not to row in front of Gary and myself, and the rows never became physical." Duncan can't put his finger on why his father started drinking, "It could have been worrying about his work, it could have been that he was missing the UK, but drink certainly started to get the better of dad." Gary would have been about 14 or 15 when it started, and his younger brother could see that it was having an adverse effect on Gary's relationship with his father. Gary was mother's boy, and he began to stand up to his father. Eventually there was a major row, with mother, father and eldest son really going at it. It was the end for the family unit. Gary had witnessed enough and didn't like what was happening, so moved out of the family home.

Within a couple of years, doctors had advised Arthur that if he continued the lifestyle he was leading, he could be dead within six months. Duncan says that the full reason for their return was never discussed; it could have been the freely available drink, the weather, the climate. He never knew. Regardless, it was decided to go back to the UK, and the Hockings – Arthur, Marjory and Duncan – boarded the Union Castle Line's *Windsor Castle* on 28th October, 1955, for the return passage, leaving Gary in Rhodesia. Even at this juncture the demon of drink surfaced. Duncan recalls that his father left the boat at one of the calls down the East African coast, only to get involved with a rowdy drinking group which resulted in him being locked overnight in a police cell. He then had to fly to another port to catch up with the *Windsor Castle* and the rest of his family.

While the rest of the family returned to the UK, Gary stayed behind to finish his apprenticeship, following his father's footsteps as a fitter and turner with the railways. When the remainder of the family returned to Wales, Gary made the decision to remain in Rhodesia to finish his education and pursue his career, and went to live with Mrs Ward, who owned a garage in Bulawayo. Her son, Ralph, was a fellow student with Gary at the high school, and even when he returned to Rhodesia many years later, he was often to be seen sitting on the counter at Ward's Transport garage talking to Mrs Ward.

Somehow, though, something went wrong with the relationship, and in his letter of October 1956 Gary mentions that "I am staying back at Kathleen's house because those Ward people made me sick with their high-minded ideas." He doesn't mention what upset him, but also shows that he had wider interests, as he asks his mother what she thinks of Roy Walenski being elected as prime minister of Rhodesia, adding that he "agrees with Eden and plans to stand with him, I mean about Egypt." The Suez war was to start less than a month later.

At some stage, Gary moved in with the Fay family. Father Richard Fay had a Triumph Tiger 110, and by now Gary's Jawa had also been traded in for a similar machine. Former classic bike racer Reg Bolton described the Tiger as "A Classic British bike, it vibrates like hell and goes quite fast. It's a road bike, they can be tuned up, but if you tune it to go faster it vibrates even more and bits fall off. It isn't the sort of bike you would say you are going to win on like a Manx Norton, but if you have someone with Gary's talent on them, then they can be a winning bike." Hocking stripped down the Jawa, rebuilt it, but then sold it because it was not big enough to satisfy his appetite for speed.

The Fays lived about 12 miles outside Bulawayo on the Khami Road. It was a large family, mainly boys, and Gary became very close friends with Richard Fay, and the two started work at Rhodesian Railways on the same day. It was a happy family atmosphere. Mrs Fay was a portly, jovial lady, always smiling and laughing, who loved to go to the local auctions. Mr Fay was a smartly dressed man who was often to be seen wearing his blazer with his army badge on the breast pocket. Nothing worried him. If a couple of the boys, including Gary, returned home late one night and had forgotten their keys, they would break a small pane of glass and get into the house. Mr Fay would say that he would go to town and get a small piece of glass to repair the damage. No problem, and that was all that would be said about the incident.

Hocking had other close friends, whom he would stick with for the rest of his life: Billy James, Ivan Rose and Johnny Evans. They weren't interested in the city life; they would prefer to head out into the bush, where one of their often-practised tricks was to drive up alongside the wildebeest and have one of them leap onto an animal's back and ride it.

Gary, like his father, became a turner. Nobby Clark takes up the story. "Where we worked they had a siren which went off at six thirty, and we used to start work at seven o'clock. Richard and Gary, having heard the siren, used to race from their house to the workshops, and they would get to the workshops and clock on just in time."

You can imagine that with two riders on similar machines riding the empty Rhodesian roads, there would no-doubt have been an element of competition between Richard and Gary on these trips into work, but this wasn't where Gary Hocking got the racing bug.

Nobby Clark remembers that, on a Saturday afternoon, 90 per cent of Bulawayo's youngsters assembled at the local cinema. The movie would end at about half past four, and then the fun would begin, recalls Clark. "All the guys with motorcycles used to race around the town, and their nickname was the 'Main Street Cowboys.'"

As the riders began to burn up the city centre, local constable Greenwood would jump onto his bike and give chase. Locals believed that he enjoyed the chase as much as the boys enjoyed giving him the run around – even if, on the rare occasions he caught one of them, it would only result in a telling off.

It was in these impromptu burn-ups around Bulawayo that Hocking was spotted by one of the well known Rhodesian riders of the time, Ken Robas. Robas advised Hocking in uncompromising language that if he wanted to kill himself riding a motorcycle, then it was better to do it on a track than on the roads. The chance to take part in something more formal than the Saturday afternoon competition against the local law enforcers obviously appealed to Hocking who, when asked what he had to do, was told by Robas to turn up at the Umgusa speedway circuit just outside Bulawayo – an invitation he accepted.

2

A helping hand

THERE COMES A time for anyone successful in their field, when they have to admit that they were in the right place at the right time, and were also given a helping hand along the way. There appear to be three elements that contributed to Gary Hocking's success. First, his own talent and determination. Second, meeting someone who could show him what to do and how to do it, and hone that talent – that was Ken Robas. And third, finding someone who could promote the talent. That was John Wells.

Robas was the Rhodesian motorcycle champion, and had started racing at the Umgusa circuit in the latter part of the 1940s. For the next ten years he tasted success, holding lap records at Umgusa and Coronation Park. He also won the most respected race in Rhodesia, the Mashonaland 100, twice in successive years: first at the Belvedere circuit and the following year at Marlborough. The second time he broke the lap record set by Bepe Castellani. Later in his career Robas would have several tussles with Hocking before the older man retired in 1960.

It was Robas who spotted Hocking as one of the Main Street Cowboys. Robas recalled the dangers of riding at speed around the streets of Bulawayo, even in the late '50s. "Racing at 60mph, there was no chance of stopping if a car came out of a side street or in the opposite direction. There were two storm drains in the Main Street, and you hit the first one at speed and leapt over the second."

Robas watched dozens of riders in those unofficial races, but there was one who stood out. "We had quite a few in the Cowboys, most of them were no-hopers, but Gary was the master." Gary and Eddie Fay (Richard's brother) both had motorbikes, and often went to the Umgusa speedway track where they could gain easy access and raced around the track. It was as a result of these impromptu races that Gary Hocking decided to have a go at racing.

With his good looks, money in his pocket from regular work, and his skill on a motorbike, you can imagine that a date with Gary Hocking was a star prize for any girl in Bulawayo, and after visiting Ken Robas' aunt's house on many occasions he began dating Robas' cousin, Kathleen, and they became close friends.

Robas didn't help only Hocking – he helped anyone who he saw had potential, but the most successful of those he took under his wing was the boy from Wales.

John Wells is an Englishman who, like so many at the time, and so many in this story, emigrated to Rhodesia. Wells had spent all his life on motorcycles since he first obtained a licence at the age of 16. Wells ran a motorcycle business, Wheelers of Newbury, and got to know top management and key men in the racing departments of most motorcycle factories, including Norton managing director Gilbert Smith, who would be of great use in the future.

Wells riding career came to an abrupt end when he was involved in a road accident and badly damaged a leg. Not to lose his connections with the sport he loved, he became involved in club life, the Auto Cycle Union, and working with people involved in running, organising, and sponsoring events and riders.

When John Wells arrived in Rhodesia in 1955 he joined the staff of Van Rooyens motorcycle works in Bulawayo, but was also keen to kickstart motorcycle racing again, which seemed to be in the doldrums. Wells was instrumental in rekindling interest in the Matabeleland Motorcycle Club. Races were organised and very quickly Wells got to know the people involved in Rhodesian motorcycling, and they got to know him. Even though Wells was only 27 he became known as the Godfather of motorcyclists. He travelled with the big name riders of the day: Jim Redman, Ken Robas, John Love, and Gary Hocking.

Wells spotted the potential of Ken Robas, and suggested that he might like to try his luck in Europe. Wells thought that Robas was potential world champion material, and, with his connections – especially Gilbert Smith in the Norton setup – he assured Robas that he could get him a Norton team ride, as Smith was changing his team due to the retirement of the three main riders.

At this time, organisers of events in Europe were glad to have an international flavour to their race programmes, but not to overload the overseas entries. So riders had to be organised and to get their entries in early in the season otherwise they would be beaten to the slot. The promoters wanted some overseas riders, but they didn't want the races flooded at the expense of Europeans, but Rhodesians such as Ray Amm and South Africans like Bepe Castellani, who had raced in Europe in 1954 and 1958, had been well-respected competitors.

The Rhodesian admitted that he would have loved to take up the opportunity, but as his wife had just delivered twins, his family commitments were the greater responsibility at the moment.

Appreciating the family ties that prevented Robas from taking up the offer of Europe, another rider took Wells' attention, and that was Gary Hocking. Wells had met Hocking previously, and knew about his riding skills.

Hocking was determined to succeed. John Wells recalled: "Gary was sitting around looking in deep thought and I asked him, 'What's up Sox?' He replied that he thought he could be as good as anyone on a motorbike. He had two arms, two legs just like anyone else, he just had to go quicker than anyone else."

What possibly makes Hocking even more of a one-off is that he was not only a good rider, but he could tune a machine, and could put the bits together to make bikes work. Wells remembered the first trip into South Africa he went on with the young Welshman and saw firsthand his skill in assembling his machine. John Wells explained: "I travelled with John Love and Gary to a race in South Africa at the Roy Hesketh Circuit, Pietermaritzburg. John had his car on the trailer at the back of the van and we took Gary's Norton along with us, but it didn't have any gearbox internals at all, just an empty shell. I asked Sox what he was going to do with it and he told me that Beppe Castellani was going to bring down a set of gears, which he did. When we arrived on the Saturday morning at Pietermaritzburg, Castellani handed over a bag of gears to Sox who put the bike on its side in the paddock and put the gearbox together. He practised, raced, won the big race, grabbed the money and we left. Love also won the car races, so with his winnings as well we were well flushed for the journey home."

Robas remembers Hocking's early sorties onto a race track. "He made an impression right away, he started racing and he went really quick. There was a meeting up in Salisbury and I couldn't go due to work commitments. The bike was set up for me, but Gary sat on it and looked comfortable. Up in Salisbury that time he won everything, and I think he even broke the lap record as well. On a bike he was a genius."

John Wells also recalls Hocking turning up at his motorcycle business dressed in a huge army greatcoat on a blazing hot day. It was October, the hottest month, and when he was asked why he was wearing a winter coat in the height of summer, he opened it up and said it was the only way he could smuggle his cylinder head into and out of the Rhodesian Railways workshop where he was working on it!

Travelling to the meetings around South Africa wasn't easy. Hocking managed to scrape enough money together to purchase a well used mark one Ford Zephyr. Once the mechanical wizard had made the vehicle roadworthy he then set about building a trailer out of a similar vehicle to carry the bikes. He visited Happy Drapers, a local scrap yard, to buy as many tyres and wheels as he could carry to fit the trailer. Why so many? Well apparently the roads around Rhodesia and South Africa at the time were so bad that secondhand tyres, probably already having travelled plenty of miles, were soon reduced to shreds. This is where good friend Eddie Fay came into his own. According to Nobby Clark, Fay was "A bull of a man." So Fay would lift the trailer including the bikes and the spare wheels, whilst Hocking would remove the worn out wheel and slip on a fresh one. "They would only do up a couple of the nuts," said Jim Redman, "as they knew that after a few miles they would have to repeat the procedure." Once secured, Fay would lower the trailer and the journey would continue. Apparently the trailer still exists out in Bulawayo.

Clarke recalls that it was something of a scramble. "We would leave work and jump in the car as we had to make the border before dusk when the crossings were closed. Once out of Rhodesia we could take it a little easier and proceed to wherever we were heading."

Ken Robas was also one of the biking travellers. "We would leave straight after work on the Friday evening and drive through the night to our destination, race, and get back for work on Monday morning. To go to Jo'burg was an 800km trip, to go to Durban, Pietermaritzburg, was a 1200km journey and we would have a two-bike trailer." It would be unheard of for a rider to travel these distances on their own, quite often a couple of them plus a friend or two would go in the van together and share the driving. It was the only way riders could get to the destinations fit enough to still ride in two or three races during the race day.

Once at their destination, with barely enough money for the journey and to fill the bikes with fuel for the races, the riders would end up sleeping in cars or vans or anywhere else where they could grab a few uncomfortable hours. Sometimes as Ken Robas recalls they were lucky enough to stay with Friends. "In Salisbury we stayed with the McDonald family, and there was another family who put us up in Pietermaritzburg, but I can't remember their name."

The riders would rely on the start money and if they were lucky their winnings to finance the trips of such long distances and failure to win races often meant scrounging enough fuel to get home again. Jim Redman recalls that meals would be a tin of beans, but if they won, then luxury they could add sausages!

Rhodesia had a remarkable record of producing racers, both on bikes and later in cars, who went on to become world champions – Bruce Beale, Ray Richards, Alan Harris, and Jim Redman, who had 45 grand prix victories from his 135 races, in addition to Gary Hocking. But the place also had race tracks, some more basic than others. In Bulawayo there was Kumalo, Falls Road, Heany (tarmac), and Umguza. In Salisbury, Belvedere, Marlborough, Coronation Park and Donnybrook. Umtali had circuits that all hosted events throughout the years, and prompted a rivalry between the fans in the two main cities of Bulawayo and Salisbury. The number of tracks shows the enthusiasm for the sport, and the fact that Rhodesia produced so much racing talent should not come as a particular surprise.

Some of these places were simply carved out of the bush by the local motorcycle club. A tractor would clear the brush and the trees before the dirt track remaining was covered with tons of old oil to keep the dust down, otherwise nobody would have seen anything, and no rider following the leader would have seen anything of the route ahead. That, though, wasn't usually a problem for Gary Hocking.

A day or so before the events took place, the local volunteers would put up their temporary pits and toilets. There might be a few safety fences where the public went, but nothing permanent. "The whole event was like a circus," said John Wells. "The local club would do everything, and the crowds would come from the city in large numbers, pay their few pence and have a great day." Pictures survive of fans who parked their cars only a few yards from the action, and took out their picnics or started their barbecues – or braai's, as the South Africans call them. The safety precautions compared with today's Formula One and MotoGP were meagre to say the least, although there would probably be a doctor in attendance and even an ambulance. Wells recalled "The events had to be run according to the local motor racing association, who would also insist on proper marshals. It wasn't a hillbilly affair, even though it may have looked like it. One week the riders would come down from Salisbury to Bulawayo, the next week they would go up to Salisbury, and that's the way it happened almost every other weekend." There was great rivalry between the two cities.

Later one or two tarmac circuits sprung up, mainly on airports or former military bases. One such was Heany in Bulawayo. The finishing straight was the runway for the airport where many of the later arrivals in Rhodesia actually landed. The local motorcycle club was allowed to come in on the Friday before the events and put up its temporary bits and pieces, but straight after the racing finished everything had to be taken down, as the aerodrome returned to its normal use. These were the places where the Rhodesian riders like Gary Hocking honed their skills, and learnt the art of motorcycle racing. Early in his career Hocking was prepared to take risks; he was prepared to take a shaving off the hay bales positioned around the track. People have called it razorblade stuff. These riders like Hocking all did their ground work on dirt circuits. They learnt their trade on tracks like Coronation Park in Salisbury, or Umgusa in Bulawayo.

There was a style associated with the dirt track riders that resembles the speedway riders of today. The rider sat very upright, with his inside foot often on the ground to help with adhesion. There was little grip from the wheels on the mixture of dirt and oil, so cornering was helped by the inside foot. The knees were pressed well against the fuel tank, with the outside foot on the foot rest.

In a letter Sox wrote home in October 1956, he tells his mother about some of his early races. "I've been racing at Umgusa speedway lately on Richard Fay's old bike. I have raced four times, last time in Salisbury in the Ray Amm memorial meeting. The second and third time I came to grief, that is fell off. I slid while passing a fella on the outside, bumping into him and causing both of us to fall. Another four fellows fell off while hitting or dodging the fallen bikes. Luckily nobody got hurt. The second time I fell off on a corner while doing about fifty odd. This time I was knocked unconscious, only for a few minutes mind you, so don't worry. Anyway don't worry probably I won't be racing until I get my new bike which is due to arrive in February or March." What Marg, his mother, must have thought when she read about his exploits would have been worth knowing, but it goes without saying that she was probably pretty concerned about her eldest son's motorbike racing.

Sox had a major fright himself before his career had even got started. He told his mother that he had received his call up papers to the Rhodesian army at Heany in the summer of 1956. "I was there for about three weeks and then I was discharged with flat feet. How do you like that? I was discharged a few days later, not that I am very sorry about it mind you."

Few records, if any, exist of the early dirt track races, and certainly nothing that gives us a clue as to Hocking's thoughts on his progress. Wells, however, saw the first time he came across the novice rider that he had a natural talent. "You could see that the fella had an exceptional talent on a motorcycle, call it flair or whatever. He just stood out from the crowd there was no doubt about it. He could jump on any motorbike and go quickly. Most young people love sheer speed whether that be on a bicycle, a skateboard, or whatever, they want to go quicker on whatever they can get. A few of them develop like Gary Hocking."

More than that Hocking had a determination added Wells, who also convinced the youngster that he had "Loads of natural talent and that he was probably the right guy to attack it. That was the way he set himself up at the start of his career, why can't he be as good as anyone else? On a motorbike Hocking was stunning. He fitted a motorcycle perfectly, and he was just bursting with natural talent ... You are so lucky to find out what you are good at at a young age, and then to brush shoulders with Ken Robas who showed you what to do and how to do it."

Many people helped Gary Hocking on his way to stardom, and many who acknowledge his achievements say how important John Wells was to his career. Wells, though, is the first to lay a lot of the credit at the door of Ken Robas. "Ken set him up in the right direction and encouraged him. He showed him what to do and how to do it. Sox latched onto me because he knew I knew the system in the UK, and I was sure I could get him into a ride over here."

The first occasion John Wells actually saw Gary Hocking ride on tarmac was in the Geoff Duke international road race meeting in Salisbury, on 24th February 1957. It happened to be Gary's very first road race, and he borrowed a 250cc Velocette from his good friend Cedric Rae. "It wasn't the fastest motorbike in Rhodesia, but he won the race straight away against a field of proven riders. He dominated the race from start to finish in a somewhat polished performance, and stood out from the crowd," recalled Wells. That was when Gary decided that he would like to go further in road racing, with a style based very much on Ken Robas. His success was instant.

Once Gary Hocking had achieved everything he could in Rhodesia and South Africa, he turned his attention to bigger things. John Wells takes up the story again: "Once he had done his apprenticeship, shall we say, in motor racing, he was determined to go ahead and go the whole way. So he gave up everything to go over there [the UK] with an empty suitcase."

Hocking approached Wells to enquire about the possibilities of racing in Europe. In Rhodesia there were no major sponsors, so there was little money to be made from motorbike racing. Here was a different challenge for 'the godfather,' as Hocking didn't have the money to finance his venture.

"He needed guidance," said Wells, "because you can't go over there and just start racing. By February everything in the UK has been oversubscribed. You have to get your programme for the whole season done early. You have to arm yourself with a fancy piece of note paper, put all your successes down the side, so you have to plan it in the right time and the right way. Sox knew he was good and he had an air of determination about him, not a bravado or an arrogance. The guys needed someone to introduce them to the big world, and that is where I came in, I became a third party. There was no money involved or anything like that." Wells had the contacts because he had been in the UK and knew the right people.

Wells suggested that he might be able to get him sponsored by a dealer friend of his, Reg Dearden in Manchester. The advantage with Dearden was that he got his hands on the previous year's works Nortons, which were the next best thing to an actual works ride.

Wells wrote to Reg Dearden: "I am writing this letter to try and help him [Hocking] achieve an ambition, mainly because I think he is more than an average rider." Wells included Hocking's list of achievements in South Africa, but had to admit that his road racing experience had only been gained over a 12 to 14 month period.

Wells also wrote to Graham Walker, who was covering the imminent Isle of Man TT races for the BBC. Wells hoped that Mr Walker would introduce Hocking to some useful contacts.

Graham Walker is the father of Murray, who is well known in the UK for his unique style of motor racing commentary. Murray began his commentating career with his father at the Isle of Man TT meetings. Graham Walker had been a brilliant rider, and winner of the Lightweight TT in 1931, amongst many other international events. He had been a despatch rider in the First World War, and later became competition manager for the Norton and Sunbeam teams, before retiring from competition racing and editing *Motor Cycling* magazine. He knew useful people in the racing game.

Unfortunately, the letter didn't reach Walker until after his return from the Isle of Man, but his reply was: "I have a feeling I met him with Jim Redman. I can recall Jim introducing me to someone whose name I didn't catch, but there was considerable noise going on. I have now come to the conclusion that it must have been poor Gary." Such was the influence, though, that Wells had with his contacts, that Graham Walker added he was now trying to find Gary Hocking's whereabouts to contact him.

John Wells was also aware at this time that it was easier to get someone like Gary introduced because the organisers liked to have a Commonwealth influence in their teams: one South African, one New Zealander, one Rhodesian, fitted the bill nicely. It was often easier to get a rider from the Commonwealth into a team than one from Great Britain, which is why letters went to Reg Dearden and Graham Walker.

John Wells is quick to play down his part in the establishment of Gary Hocking in Europe, explaining that all he did was act as a middle man. "I simply acted as a third party," said Wells. "It was easier for me to come into your office and say I know Gary Hocking, he is a very talented motorcyclist. That was easier than you going in and saying I'm Gary Hocking and I am bloody good on a motorbike. Also I knew the channels over here." There was no money involved; in fact, Wells said that he had tried to get people in Rhodesia to help young Hocking financially, without success.

Wells was concerned that by the time Hocking had approached him it was too late in the year to be planning on going to England, or rather the Isle of Man. It was May and the TT was in June and by that time all the teams had gathered their riders and were well established. The only hope was someone like Reg Dearden.

One rider who had returned to England from Rhodesia and was already amongst that established group was Jim Redman. He also paved the way for Gary Hocking to make a name for himself in Europe. Redman had sold his motorcycle business in preparation for his return for the 1958 season in Europe, but to fill time before his departure he had set up a lean-to workshop behind the business owned by Mick Gammon in Bulawayo. Gammon was quite happy for Redman to do the repairs, which fitted in nicely with his motorcycle sales.

When Redman was ready to leave for Europe, he said to Gary Hocking "Why don't you take over my business?" Hocking accepted, and left the railways to work for himself as a motorcycle mechanic. Redman said he was a very clever guy, a brilliant mechanic, and a brilliant tuner, which was a major asset to him in later years.

Redman had a couple of races in South Africa before he left, jumping on the boat in Cape Town, and heading for England to pick up his Nortons. His first race meeting was at Brands Hatch, where he had a tremendous tussle with the 'King of Brands,' Derek Minter. After the races Redman was asked about his event, and whether he realised that he had almost beaten Derek Minter, to which Redman replied "Derek who?"

Redman was now big news back in Rhodesia having almost beaten Minter, and when Gary Hocking heard that he had come second he was reported to have said, "Shit, I would have won it, I had better go." Hocking went to the local bazaar, brought a cardboard suitcase, filled it with all his belongings and £200, which was all he had in the world, caught a plane to England, and eventually arrived at the Isle of Man on the eve of the TT where, according to Redman, he said "Give me a bike."

John Wells recalls the day his friends saw off Gary to Europe. "It was the 26th of May 1958. The previous day Gary had won the big race at the Heany National Meeting on a 650 Ridgeback. He had only his leathers, helmet, a wash bag and little else. His suitcase rattled!

Redman also followed the route of writing to Reg Dearden and others, asking for sponsorship, but was turned down. But following his success against Derek Minter at Brands Hatch the situation changed, and Dearden, amongst others, was willing to sponsor Redman. Redman, though, was being given other advice that his bikes appeared to be going well, so why commit to a sponsor who would dictate where and what he rode, when as a freelance he could pick and choose to suit himself? So Redman suggested to Dearden that, as his bikes were going so well, "Don't sponsor me, sponsor Sox – he's better than me."

"Little did I know what would happen," Redman added.

Hocking is very likely to have met with Reg Dearden at the 1958 Isle of Man TT, but, with so much involvement in the races and his bikes, the meeting meant little to Dearden, and the letters from John Wells had been forgotten. Hocking, though, was determined, and the next meeting came at Dearden's shop in Manchester. Reg's son, Nigel, was ten at the time Hocking appeared at the counter. His description of his father's premises fits nicely with the recollection of George Costain, who also knew the building. "318 Barlow Moore Road Chorlton-Cum-Hardy Manchester," said George with a chuckle. "He had so much stuff there that if you had a cup of tea there wasn't enough room to put the cup down! It was absolutely ram jam packed tight full." Nigel said it was nothing like the sanitised showrooms you go into these days. "There was a small counter, then behind that a workbench covered with parts, and the bikes were lined up down the sides. If you wanted a bike you were told to go and pick out the one you wanted." Reg preferred to be tinkering with the parts and pieces.

Hocking appeared one day, and asked Reg Dearden to lend him two bikes, because, he said, "I am going to become the world champion." Something of a shock to Reg, who suggested something along the lines of 'Certainly, and the rest of the world as well!' Hocking, though, wasn't for giving up – he played his trump card, producing the return half of his ticket to South Africa. "That's all I have," he said, "if you don't help me."

This was beginning to pull Dearden's heart strings, who asked Hocking where he was staying, and, of course, the answer was "Nowhere." So Dearden arranged a test to see how good this cocky little fellow from South Africa really was, and took a couple of bikes to Oulton Park, the local track. Dearden soon had his answer. Within half a dozen laps Hocking was turning in close to lap record times, and Dearden had only one thing to say – "Son, I'll help you."

Such was the accommodating nature of the Deardens that Nigel's bedroom was moved around for the umpteenth time and Sox shared a room with him for the best part of two years. Nigel recalls that every night Gary read a book before he went to sleep, and that book was the bible.

Hocking was in his element, and apart from riding the bikes he began making his own from the parts available. The theory was that the running gear on a bike was down to the rider's preference, but the engine was down to Dearden. Gary, of course, wasn't happy with this, and began questioning his host, who got so fed up with his constant chirping away about bikes, setups and tuning, that he just said "Right, go ahead, take to bits you want and build a Manx Norton. I will build one as well and we will see which is best." At the test at Olton Park, Gary rode his and then Dearden's, but was forced to admit that Dearden's was the better machine.

Bob Dowty and George Costain knew Dearden, and rode his bikes. Dowty remembers that the Manchester dealer was a larger-than-life character, and Costain called him a "likeable rogue," but one thing most people agree on was that Dearden helped Gary Hocking establish himself on the international motor racing circuit, and enabled him to develop his career.

Dearden started out as a butcher, but after building up a number of shops he became fed up with the meat trade and gave it up for his love of bikes. He made his money just after the war when the British economy was on its knees. British car manufacturers had to make sure they exported most, if not all their new cars to help the balance of payments. One place they could export to was Eire, the Republic of Ireland. As it was so difficult to buy a new car in the UK, Dearden would import cars from Eire and sell them to his customers and contacts.

He was also a keen motorcycle racer, and raced either side of the Second World War, but, as Bob Dowty recalls, he was not in the same class as Gary Hocking. "He had a 'harum scarum' attitude to racing, he didn't take the professional attitude, he just went out and blasted the bike. He took the corners as he vaguely remembered them and came off umpteen times." Dearden had other attributes though; he liked women, but also liked good riders. George Costain remembers his first meeting with the man who, he said, "could sell a fridge to an Eskimo. He was very, very good to me. I first met Reg Dearden when I rode in the Manx Grand Prix in 1953. He introduced himself and asked 'What are your plans for next year?'" Costain explained that he didn't know his plans as he didn't have a bike. "Don't you worry about a bike," said Dearden, "I'll make sure you get a bike." Costain recalls that Dearden would go out on the early morning practices and look out for riders he thought would suit his machines.

"Reg Dearden either took a liking to you or he didn't. He took to Gary Hocking, and then to learn the TT he had Gary shipped over to the Isle of Man and he stayed with me for a month or two in the winter. It was so cold, poor Gary nearly sat on the fire, he was so cold."

Bob Dowty agrees with Costain's assessment of Dearden, but adds that you couldn't help but like the guy. "He was a very good tuner of motorbikes when he put his mind to it. The trouble was that he brought over so many bikes and had so many riders that they were all looking to him to tune their bike, but, of course because he was doing so many other things he never got around to half of them, but he did look after his top two or three riders." One year he had no fewer than 22 machines on the island and was servicing nine riders.

Motorbikes were also subject to restrictions on the sale in the UK, but in those days, with a little sweetener here or there, it was possible to jump the queue and get machines, which Reg did with great success. As Bob Dowty says, "Reg had his ways."

There can be no doubt that once Gary had arrived in England, established himself with Reg Dearden and with his own talent, the pieces were in place for his career to progress. Dearden played no small part in the road to success ridden by Gary Hocking. He helped the youngster, as he had helped many before him and would continue to after. Reg Dearden's place in motorcycle history should not be underestimated.

3

The tracks and the bikes

GARY HOCKING HAD taken the advice, forsaking the storm drains of Bulawayo and the Saturday afternoon chase with the local police, and was ready to pit his skills on the tracks of South Africa. There was a tremendous enthusiasm for motorsport in Rhodesia – the number of tracks around the country and further afield in South Africa emphasised the fact.

No rider was ever going to make a fortune riding bikes in South Africa, but prize monies of 20 pounds here and there would make the long journeys not only worthwhile, but also financially viable. Even though some riders got appearance money, life was a great deal easier if the races were won, and if Gary Hocking was in it, he was in it to win it. The young wizard won several scratch and handicap races on the dirt circuits, which proved to be the basis of his racing education.

He had learnt the basics on the dirt tracks of Umgusa in Bulawayo and Coronation Park in Salisbury, which were the breeding grounds for Rhodesian riders. That style of racing Hocking would take with him to the road circuits as so many had done before him. He had traded in his trusty Triumph Tiger 100 in part exchange for a new Tiger 110.

On 24th February 1957, Hocking was ready to take the plunge in the wider world, and entered the Geoff Duke International Road Race Meeting in Salisbury, southern Rhodesia. The meeting took place at the Belvedere circuit.

There had been a previous circuit at Belvedere, the road circuit, which traversed the roads around the old horse race course. The course had storm drains across several areas, which were filled in for the race meetings, and apparently was quick, too. But this race was held at the new circuit, which had been built later, on the site of the air base.

The track was two miles (3.219km) in length, the riders or drivers going around in a clockwise direction, but according to some riders it was a boring track for both competitors and spectators alike, being fairly simple with nothing really outstanding about it. The start and finish line was on a slight bend, before the riders went into a much sharper bend and onto the main straight. There was one long straight on the airport runway known as Pichanie Street, which they tried to make more interesting by putting in a chicane. This straight was slightly uphill, so you could never reach the top speed that you could on the back straight, which was slightly downhill. Here riders could get near the 100mph mark, but this was difficult to confirm, as racing bikes in those days didn't have speedometers. Because so much of the track was on a straight line there were plenty of passing opportunities for the faster riders, of which no doubt Gary Hocking was one. He won on all four occasions he rode there during 1957.

Newspaper previews of the event predicted an excellent entry and some high speeds, and, like the majority of meetings held around that time, there were both motorbike and car events. In this case 50 bikes and 34 cars would line up, and to whet the appetite of the locals – if such a thing was needed – names were dropped into articles, including those of current world champion Geoff Duke, plus Dave Chadwick, who had both come over from England together. Apart from the two big names, there were 37 entries in either the car or bike races from Salisbury, plus ten from Bulawayo, including, of course, Gary Hocking – yet to be worthy of a name drop to attract supporters through the gates. A turnout of 25,000 was expected for the races, which, the newspaper preview assured the fans, would go ahead "regardless of the weather," which must have been an issue at the time.

There were due to be 11 250cc machines, which would include Hocking on the 250cc Velocette with a megaphone exhaust, which had been loaned to him by occasional racer Cedric Wray, who was also a friend of Ken Robas and John Wells. The Velocette was probably built about 1949, but had been extensively modified by Mike Towell. It was a straightforward standard model, which riders at the time would convert into a racing machine. Hocking no-doubt 'fiddled' with the settings to get the best out of the aged machine.

Neither the local newspaper's preview nor the race report in *Motorcycle News* regarded Hocking as worthy of a mention. All the talk was of Duke, and the fact that he had unveiled a memorial to Ray Amm in Ray Amm Avenue. The ceremony was attended by cabinet ministers and the Mayor of Salisbury.

"Another triumphant appearance," stated the January 27th 1957 issue of *Motorcycle News*, as Duke won the 500cc scratch event on a Gilera, five yards ahead of Castellani. Dave Chadwick was described as one of the stars of the meeting following his win in the 350cc event on a streamlined Norton. There was no mention of our hero Hocking, despite him guiding the Velocette to first place in the 250cc event, leaving the rest of the field in his wake.

Two months later, Hocking was back at the Belvedere circuit for the Salisbury Motorcycle and Light Car Club national meeting. This time Hocking had his hands on a 350cc Norton, which Ken Robas recalls he loaned to Sox on this occasion. Another 350cc short-stroke Norton was to be the machine that Hocking rode for the remainder of 1957, with almost total success, but where Sox got this particular Norton from is a mystery. John Wells thought initially it was one of Ken Robas' machines, but Ken said that, although he lent one to Sox for the first meeting, this one wasn't his. Another theory put forward by Shaun Robinson suggested it could have come from John Emms, as at this time Emms was moving on from bikes to cars. This theory is again blown out of the water, as it's thought Emms rode a 500cc Norton rather than a 350cc.

How Gary Hocking really came by the Norton came to light just as I was packing everything together to send off to the publisher. An email landed in my inbox from Rodger Gilson, in Pretoria. He had come across a *South Wales Argus* online article about the book, and had some exciting news. The email was followed by a letter sent from Gilson's father, Ivor. Ivor loved old British motorbikes, and had restored many machines, including a Vincent Comet that he exchanged for a partly restored and shabby looking Manx Norton. The owner of the Norton, by the name of Jim Carter, believed the machine to have been ridden by Gary Hocking, and he produced a pouch of documents detailing the history of the machine, including confirmation of the engine number from the Norton Owners' Club. The machine had been sold new to a garage owner in Surrey by the name of Sadler. After racing the machine on the Isle of Man, Sadler sold it to John Love, who owned a garage in Bulawayo. Presumably when he moved into cars, John Love later sold or gave the Norton to Gary Hocking.

Carter had acquired the machine from the estate of a John D'Olivera, who had been a reporter on *The Bulawayo Chronicle* covering Hocking's rise to fame. The two became close friends, and D'Olivera either purchased the machine directly from Gary, or brought it from Gary's estate after he died.

With the troubles brewing in Rhodesia, D'Olivera got the bike and himself out of the country and took up a post as motoring correspondent for a newspaper in Pretoria. A chance meeting between Gilson and D'Olivera resulted in Gilson being invited to see D'Olivera's bikes in his garage. Gilson said that when he went into the garage his eyes nearly popped out of his head, as tucked away in a corner was a Manx Norton with a yellow racing plate and black numbers. It was complete, but obviously had been well used. Very soon after the meeting, D'Olivera died suddenly of a heart attack, so the relationship ended, as did Gilson's interest in the bike, until his contact with Carter.

The swap between the Vincent and the Norton took place, and Ivor Gilson takes up the story. "Having got the Manx home, I had a close look at it and was horrified as it had no brake shoes and no primary chain guard. The back wheel rim aluminum alloy flange had serious cracks. However, it had a good condition Dunlop racing tyre on it. Things got worse after removing the large aluminium petrol tank. I lifted the cam box and cylinder head – no cams, no vertical drive and no bevel gears, as well as no cam followers [buckets], but new racing quality valves were fitted with hair springs. The cylinder had a brand new sleeve bored and honed with a brand new Manx piston and rings. I removed the engine from the frame and dismantled it, and to my delight I found it had a brand new state of the art conrod and crankpin, plus a brand new main roller and ball bearings. It was very obvious to me a motor engineering firm had done a very good job on the above mentioned bits."

Gilson got to work sourcing the parts necessary to restore the machine to its 1956 condition, and it was whilst he was doing this that he noticed on the underside of the barrel head that the word 'Hocking' had been scratched into the metal.

Ivor Gilson is keen to add that he is not saying 100 per cent that this is Hocking's bike, but given the evidence he has and the research he has undertaken, he says: "I personally believe this is Gary Hocking's racing bike, and will stick by it."

Speaking to other people who were around at the time, there is debate both for and against the claim. Obviously the engine number (10M69364) and the confirmation from the Norton Owners' Club is strong. Also, Nobby Clark says that if the engine number and the frame number match, that is almost unique. Unfortunately the frame number can't be deciphered. Then there is the name 'Hocking' scratched on the engine part. John Wells contributes by saying that, although Gary was a good mechanic and tuner, he wouldn't have had the equipment to undertake major engineering work, so he would send a job like that to Ray Murray Engineering. Either Gary scratched the name on there to make sure he got his part back, or Murray scratched it on to make sure it went back to the right person. Certainly Ivor Gilson confirms that a major engineering job had been done on the engine, and it had been done by an expert. Conversely, as privateers the riders had to repair their own bikes if they had an accident or a breakdown. They could very easily source spare parts from other machines. A different engine could have been placed into a different frame.

Wells thinks that after racing at Pietermaritzburg in January 1958, Hocking felt the Norton required refurbishment, so he began to strip it down before realising that his money would be better spent travelling to Europe, meaning the job was never completed. Hence it simply sat in the back of a garage until being purchased by D'Olivera after Gary's death. I don't think for one moment that anyone has tried to provide false information – they would have no cause to – but like all the investigation into the Gary Hocking story, it concerns events from over sixty years ago. Memories fade.

Regardless of where it came from, by now our man was on a proper racing bike: a Manx Featherbed Norton. This was the most famous Norton ever produced, and the name came about quite by accident, one of those throwaway lines. The original Norton works racing bike was rebuilt in the 1950s using a new design tubular steel frame. During testing at Silverstone, Norton works rider Harold Daniell remarked that riding the new bike was like riding on a featherbed. Shock absorbers from a motor car were used to soften the ride originally, but later, special purpose-built equipment was produced. The name stuck. The Featherbed frame was produced for the 350s and 500s, but as the frame was important in the handling of the bike – especially for the larger machine – the tubes for the 500cc were slightly larger. Such was the impact of the Featherbed that experts at the time wrote that it would take its place in motorcycle engineering history.

Geoff Duke won the 350cc and 500cc world titles on a Featherbed in 1951, and the 350cc title in 1952, so it was a natural progression for the ambitious young Hocking to go for this famous bike.

He won the SMC and LCC national meeting at the Salisbury aerodrome from a scratch start, and the following month, May 1957, he took the new Norton to the Heany 100 national meeting, back at Heany junction in Bulawayo.

"Disappointing" was the headline in the local paper the following day. "About 10,000 spectators went to Heany yesterday for thrill, speed, and (possibly) spills; in place of excitement they got sunburn," went the report. The blame lay with the handicapping, which turned every race into a procession. In the big race, the Heany 100, the big names – Castellani, Redman, Driver and Robas – were too heavily handicapped, and never had a chance of beating the handicapper on the ten-lap race. That was to the advantage, though, of Gary Hocking, who came second behind Basil Scheepers. Tommy Robinson was third on a 500cc matchless, and Ken Robas managed to get up to fifth. The highlight of the race was the duel between Redman and Driver, who went hell for leather trying to win despite their handicap.

If that was the duel of the day, the performance of the day came in the 350cc scratch race. The report reads: "A newcomer to big-time racing, Hocking of Bulawayo caused an upset in the 350 scratch by beating veterans Castellani, Wolff, and Redman. Hocking rode his Norton like an expert." Gary covered the 22.5-mile course in 19 minutes 46.8 seconds. That was only 1.6 seconds slower than Castellani's time in winning the 500cc race.

A week later Hocking was back in action, this time at the Union Day races in Peitermarizburg.

Like so many towns in South Africa, motorsport had a huge following. There was the NMCC, Natal Motorcycle and Car Club, the MMCC Maritzburg Motorcycle and Car Club, and the Parkhill Light Car Club. The latter of those three became mainly interested in side car racing, but due to lack of new machines, and lack of interest, the PLCC fell by the wayside.

Racing in Pietermarizburg used to be held at the Alexandra Park circuit, which was based on the streets. As traffic, noise and other considerations became an issue, it was decided by a group of volunteers to build a new track. The aerial photograph on page 49 shows houses quite close to the track, but when it was built it was a considerable distance from any buildings.

The land was provided by the council. Previously it been an Italian prisoner of war camp, and was far enough out of the main town to be free from any complaints. It was named the Roy Hesketh Circuit, after the famous South African motor ace who was killed in the Second World War. His father, a baker, provided a significant amount of finance to get the project off the ground, and made a rule that the gates should never be shut, which did encourage a few of the locals to take to the course for some 'unofficial' races. It was planned originally to be 1.75 miles in length, but was eventually built at 1.66 miles, and the first meeting was held there in December 1953.

A description was printed in *The Sports Car*, which described a long straight passing Henry's Knee with a fairly sharp downhill bend called Quarry Corner, or Quarry Curve. This led to a back straight known as the Pietermaritzburg, or PMB straight, which ended with a corner described as "interesting," known as the Link. The track then turned left and uphill, followed by a long right-hand bend leading to the Visitors' Straight, culminating in a long left-hand bend re-entering the main straight at the Angels Angle. This was a favourite place for the spectators, as there were always plenty of incidents here with both the bikes and the cars.

The most difficult part of the circuit was the Link, which is almost 90 degrees, and apparently was more difficult to negotiate for the bikes than the cars. Generally, though, the circuit, which went anticlockwise, was said to be a favourite with bikers, although the weather could sometimes be an issue – in some places it would be fine, but without any warning it could be raining in other sections. The article concludes by saying that the Roy Hesketh is a "Very interesting circuit."

All the big names raced there, including Mike Hailwood, Geoff Duke, Jim Redman, as well as Gary Hocking. It was said that the track 'sorted the men from the boys,' with local riders having a big advantage, and presumably Hocking was termed a local.

Another problem for riders and drivers alike at the Hesketh was the surface, which wasn't very smooth. Apparently the tyres would collect a mixture of the oil and rubber on the track, and adhesion often became a problem. After the race this sticky mass became difficult to remove from machines, and had to be almost chiselled away.

The Link, as it was known, led to the rise up Beacon Hill, which the riders would take at about 60mph. Later the Link was taken away, making the run up Beacon Hill faster. On the straights speeds would get up to a little over the 100mph mark.

Following his win at Heany against some of the top names, Hocking had started to become noticed, but at the Union Day meeting in Pietermaritzburg Gary became headline news. The race report in *The Car* magazine of July 1957 carried the headline "New motorcylce racing star comes to light."

Leonard Hill began his report with the glowing prediction: "A new motor racing star flashed across the scene. He is 19-year-old Gary Hocking of Bulawayo, an apprentice fitter and turner." Hill continued by writing that "riding a 350cc Norton he 'walked off' with both the 350 and 500cc scratch races, and was robbed of a hat-trick in the 55-mile Handicap race by engine trouble."

Hill commented that Hocking rode with a style "generally based on that displayed by Geoff Duke, giving an indication that Hocking had studied the world champion closely."

In the Handicap race, Gary had a tremendous battle with first of all Alec Grier, and later Dave Clark, both South Africans, and both far more experienced than the 19-year-old from Bulawayo. First Grier dropped out three quarters of the way through the race, but then the Norton developed engine trouble, and Hocking was forced out of the race, and thus denied a clean sweep of wins.

Hocking couldn't have had much time to repair the problem, which the magazine report put down to clutch trouble, before starting the 500cc Handicap race. Again, Hocking excelled, lapping at around 1 minute 24 seconds and pulling up to fifth place. By the 21st lap of 55, he was right up to leader Gary Burgess, before taking the lead a lap later. With nine laps to go and Sox holding a comfortable lead, the Norton suffered a recurrence of the mechanical trouble, and he had to retire.

There followed more brisk work with the tools before, first of all, the 350cc scratch race started. This time there were no problems. Hocking led from the start, and although he lost the lead from the seventh lap until the 28th, there was seldom any doubt who would eventually win. He overtook the leader, Wilmott, who was later forced to pull out, and was never headed again.

Finally the 500cc scratch event, and again there was praise from the experts as Hocking, on the same 350cc Norton, led the field from start to finish. "He overwhelmed the bigger men from the start with his tremendous speed and riding ability." That observation was backed up by riders such as Shaun Robinson, who said that the 500cc machine should always win over a 350. "Obviously the 500 has a bigger engine, it is more powerful and is faster. So for a 350 machine to beat 500 machines in a scratch race it has to be down to rider ability. Sox must have been a bloody good rider." It was the first time that Hocking had made his mark outside Rhodesia.

John Wells travelled a great deal in those early days with Sox, Ken Robas and John Love, and Wells recalls yet another Hocking story from the first trip back from Pietermaritzburg. "We were travelling all night and it was Sox's turn to drive, so John Love went to sleep in the back of the van, and I stayed up front with Gary. The last instructions John left with Gary were 'Don't push it because it's an old van,' 1939 or something like that. I had a sleep in the front as well, and when I woke up a very excited Sox said to me 'Hey, we've just done 60 miles in exactly 60 minutes.' As he said that there was a big explosion and the fan went through the radiator. John Love came to the front like a rat up a drain pipe, but I never told him what Sox had said but he wasn't too popular for the rest of that trip, and we got home two days later."

If the wider world of motorcycle racing hadn't heard of Gary Hocking, he was certainly now on the radar in South Africa. Four meetings and five wins – a run that continued at the national meeting back in Salisbury, of which we have no records, but Hocking again won the 350cc scratch race, as well as the Salisbury international meeting at the same venue.

By now Hocking was beginning to be mentioned in the preview articles along with the more established names. On Saturday August 31st 1957, *The Rhodesia Herald* announced: "More speed, bigger thrills expected at tomorrow's Mashonaland 100 meeting." This was the colony's most prestigious race meeting. Again, it was a mixture of bikes and cars, with over 40 machines expected to take part and "a bumper crowd" anticipated.

The Herald continued: "The 350cc field of 13 machines sees most of the stars together in what should be a great scratch race, especially between the Norton Featherbeds of Wolff, Hocking, Castellani and Henderson, all capable of averaging 78mph." Needless to say, Hocking lived up to his 'star billing,' and won the 350cc scratch to continue his winning streak.

Hocking's first defeat came in Johannesburg in October of 1957 at Grand Central, and it proved to be ironic that the man who beat him was the one who initially did so much to get him started in racing: Ken Robas. John Wells says that when these two raced together it was one mighty tussle, but one would win, the other would come second, and on this occasion the spoils would go to the senior man, Robas. Hocking, as usual by now, was on his tried and trusted Manx Norton, whilst Robas had moved on from his Triumph T110 and was riding an AJS 7R.

AJS was a Wolverhampton-based firm, which had been started by Albert John Stevens back around the start of the 1900s. In 1931 it was taken over by the London company Matchless to form Associated Motorcycles, and it built its machines in Woolwich, south east London. With big support for both the makes, it was decided to keep both names on their production models. The AJS 7R was the company's most popular single cylinder 350cc, which was introduced in 1948 and known affectionately as the Boy Racer. It was a hugely successful machine, and very competitive at international level. The van Rooyens Motorcycle works had brought the 7R to Bulawayo, and Robas was particularly keen to get his hands on it.

Grand Central was the least loved of the tracks by both the two-wheel and four-wheel speedsters, as it had a reputation for being bumpy. Bobby Dixon also recalls that the track was uneven, and became known as the machine breaker, although it did play an important part in the story of motor racing in South Africa ...

Again, it was built on the site of an aerodrome that was owned by an English businessman, Harry Shires, who had emigrated to South Africa. After the Second World War ended, realising the enthusiasm for motor racing, Shires allowed the construction of a 2.5-mile race track on part of the aerodrome. The track was leased by Grand Central Speedway Ltd, which staged the first event at the track in November 1949.

The venue didn't attract many spectators, and losses were soon incurred, so much so that the owners went bankrupt. This could well explain why the track was allowed to deteriorate. In an attempt to make the track faster – and no-doubt more appealing to the spectators – changes were made in the late 1950s, but the Hocking/Robas event in October 1957 would have been on the original circuit.

The changes did away with the slowest part of the track, which included Tombstone Corner and the Esses. So, the section between the Horseshoe and Total Turn now became straighter and much faster, reducing the length of the circuit to just over two miles.

Eventually the conditions of the track became too bad for cars or bikes, and after protests from riders – and especially car drivers whose vehicles were being damaged by the poor surface – Grand Central closed its doors in August 1961.

Wells recalls that Robas was another of Rhodesia's natural riders, and he was a highly rated motorcyclist. "He just looked right on a motorbike, and came with a good pedigree." He was of Greek descent, and Wells recalls he occasionally ribbed him that "... sometimes he rode smooth like a Greek Goddess, sometimes he rode like a god damn Greek!" He remembered one trip with Robas, and possibly Gary Hocking as well, when they were going to Grand Central. "We had just crossed the border into South Africa, and we were travelling on peanuts for money. We had borrowed his father's panel van, and soon after crossing the border Ken said 'This thing is gobbling petrol.' The next thing, I saw Ken pour a couple of pints of engine oil into the petrol tank. I asked him what he was doing and he said he was thickening the petrol up a bit to make it go further. I just laughed," said Wells, "but I tell you what – it did. I couldn't believe it."

Still in the early days of track racing, Robas was the master – but only just. He remembered the race day at Grand Central, which was between Johannesburg and Pretoria. "It was quite a tricky track, but a pretty one, and Gary and I practised together. Gary had acquired a 350 Norton from somewhere, I don't know how or where he got hold of it. I had just changed from a Norton to an AJS," said Robas. "In the race he followed me around for a couple of laps, and then we were racing. I beat him by about half a wheel, but only because he was trailing me for those early laps."

Two weeks after Grand Central, the master and his pupil were up against each other once more, this time in Bulawayo in the Heany Summer Handicap. Again, it would be Hocking fighting out the spoils with Robas in a shoulder-to-shoulder, leather-to-leather battle, although this time Hocking got the better of his tutor. Ken Robas remembers these two races, "two of the most fun races I ever rode, as we swapped places all the way."

The final race of 1957 came on December 15th back at Roy Hesketh in Pietermaritzburg. *Car* magazine of February 1958 carried a report of the races, and a photograph of Hocking on his 350cc Norton with the caption: "Gary Hocking, the brilliant young Rhodesian rider."

Hocking liked the Roy Hesketh course, and he showed that his efforts there six months previously were no flash in the pan. He was branded South Africa's most promising young rider of the moment. 30 riders went to the start for the 55-mile National Motorcycle Handicap, on a variety of machines of various sizes. Beppe Castellani was on a 500cc Norton, compared to a WR Collison on a 250cc Velo. Ken Robas was on his AJS and Jim Redman on another 500cc Norton.

There was a full 8 minutes and 30 seconds between the first rider away and the scratch man, Castellani, and after 11 laps the lead off riders hadn't been challenged. Dave Chadwick had fallen off at the Link, and a duel started between Castellani and Stan Setaro. Nine laps later, Gary was making a charge. He had moved up to fourth as Setaro was involved in a spectacular 100mph crash, which thankfully caused him only a few scrapes and bruises. The handicap was once again too much for Castellani. He chased the smaller machines to the finish line, but couldn't catch the flyer from Bulawayo, who was apparently riding "effortlessly and precisely." Gary took the 100 guinea prize money, with Castellani second, Robas third and Redman fourth.

In the third race of the day, engine trouble again appeared to hamper Hockings performance, the report in *Car* magazine reading that "Hocking appeared to go around at little more than three-quarter throttle and was never in the hunt."

Mike Hailwood had featured in the latter races of 1957 and early '58, and in January 1958 he would go to the start at the Fairfield Races at Pietermaritzburg, along with English colleague Dave Chadwick. Once again it was a mixture of cars and bikes, with the bike entry this time far dwarfing the entries with four wheels. The main motorcycle race was of national standing; the 45-mile Centenary Handicap with a first prize of £45. The race was a story of mishaps, with riders dropping out, and, in the case of Hocking, a fall at Angels Angle, though he was thankfully unhurt.

Whether the fall had an unsettling effect on Sox is unknown, but in the 350cc scratch race he came up against Dave Chadwick on his 350cc Norton, and Ken Robas presumably on his AJS 7R. Hocking did lead on the first lap, but when Chadwick put in a lap time of 1 minute 20 seconds and an average speed of 75mph, he gained the lead and never lost it. As the race progressed, Robas overtook Hocking, who had to be content with third place behind Chadwick and Robas. According to the reports, the 7500 spectators were treated to a series of events that kept them fully entertained. That would be Hocking's last race on his 350cc Norton.

The success Hocking had tasted progressing from the 250cc Velocette to the Norton was presumably satisfying and frustrating in equal measure. On the 350cc he proved to be virtually unbeatable, and he had won against 500cc machines – but that must have been a struggle, and taken all his skill and guts to achieve. Gary hankered after a more powerful machine to compete with the bigger bikes on more equal terms. The trusted Norton was sold to another local rider, Willie van

Leeuwan. He continued to race the bike occasionally, but never had the success on it which Hocking had enjoyed.

Three months after the January meeting at Pietermaritzburg, Hocking met up again with John Love, who would become more famous for his achievements in cars than on bikes. But Love was something of a mechanic and had put a 650 Triumph engine into a Manx Norton frame. According to those around at the time, Love had made a super job of the marriage, and as it was a 'mixture of breeds,' they decided to name it after the famous dog in Rhodesia that is also a mixture of breeds, the Rhodesian Ridgeback – derived from animals bred in Bulawayo by a Reverend Charles Helm, and in Matebeleland by a hunter called Cornelius van Rooyen.

Love offered the ride to Hocking who accepted and entered the Salisbury International Road race in the unlimited class. The meeting on the Belvedere circuit was organised to raise funds to send a Rhodesian team to the 1958 Empire Games being held ironically in Cardiff, in Hocking's homeland of Wales. Southern Rhodesia would be one of 35 nations travelling to Cardiff, and they returned with three bronze medals. William Jackson won bronze in the bowls singles, whilst Hector Philp and William Yuill gained their medals in the pairs.

It is presumed that Hocking had time to practise on the Ridgeback, but in racing conditions he took to it in his usual style: race from the front and win. It would have worked, but for an unfortunate mechanical failure when, out in front, and anticipating the chequered flag, a plug lead came loose half a lap from the finish line. That let his old friend and foe Bepe Castellani into the winning position, with Hocking struggling home in second place.

No mechanical problems a month later, when Hocking took the Ridgeback to the Heany national meeting – he scorched home ahead of Ken Robas on his Norton. However, the Bulawayo Flyer was about to sprout wings of a different kind. Destination: Europe.

A month later John Love sold the Ridgeback to a local rider, Alex MacDonald, for £125.

Hocking had startled the motorcycle fraternity in South Africa, and was already being mentioned in the same breath as some of the elite riders, including the great Ray Amm. One newspaper was bold enough to state that Hocking was already "... better than the great Ray." Following his return to Wales, Arthur Hocking told a local newspaper from his home in Canal Street, Newport, that when they were about to return home, "Gary had only just started to take an interest in motorbikes and since then he has certainly shaken them up over there."

It was time to look for a bigger challenge. Hocking had done his apprenticeship in motorcycle racing, and once he had done that, said John Wells, "... he was determined to go all the way and make good."

4
Off to Europe

Encouraged by his success in Rhodesia and South Africa, and the encouragement he had received from the likes of Ken Robas, Gary Hocking decided that his future, and possibly his fame and fortune, lay in Europe.

John Wells had already set the wheels in motion, as he promised he would, by sending letters to two of his contacts in England: Reg Dearden and Graham Walker.

Wells wrote to Dearden on May 21st 1958, explaining that a young Rhodesian rider named Gary Hocking was intending to come to the UK:

Dear Mr Dearden,

Recently I wrote to Mr Graham Walker on behalf of a young Rhodesian motorcyclist named Gary Hocking, who is at the moment here in Bulawayo and intends to come to the UK on the 30th of this month with the hope that some kind Dealer Entrant such as yourself will give him the chance to race in England or on the Continent.

From Mr Walker's reply I was given to understand that my letter had been forwarded to you and that perhaps you might consider him with a try. As I mentioned in my first letter to Mr Walker, I am writing for this rider purely to try to help him achieve his ambition, mainly because I feel he is more than just an average rider, this would certainly be confirmed by any of our riders who are in the island this year, if you can manage to have a few words with them – Castellani, Des Wolff, Paddy Driver, or Jim Redman and I am sure they will also tell you that I am not just a fan of Hocking's, if you mention my name.

Gary Hocking is 20 years of age, very light in build, and is a fitter and turner by trade, though at the moment runs a motorcycle workshop here in Bulawayo which was formerly run by Jim Redman until he left for the UK recently.

Apart from short circuit dirt riding, Gary's road racing experience is of only 12 or 14 months and I enclose a full list of his meetings for your information, he has of course won or has been placed in many handicap events but I feel they are of no importance as far as you would be concerned. The competition at most of these meetings has been good and in most cases the following riders have been present, Dave Chadwick UK Olle Rygren Sweden, Borro Castellani SA, J Stander SA, Ken Robas Rhodesia, Jim Redman Rhodesia, Paddy Driver SA, Des Wolff Rhodesia.

However there is so little time before Gary leaves for the UK and no doubt you are extremely busy at the TT time I hope you won't mind if I tell him to at least contact you somewhere in the UK or in the island as your advice alone would be of such help to this young rider.

Here's wishing you personally every success with your entries in the TT and hoping you may be able to help assist young Hocking in the future.

Yours faithfully

KJ Wells

Wells also wrote to Graham Walker on 21st May 1958, telling him about the very promising Rhodesian who was riding in the Heany 100 and then leaving for the UK to attend the Isle of Man TT. Wells continued, "I hope you will agree with me that this young rider Hocking is good when you have seen him race. I'm sure if you mention the name Hocking to our riders in the island they will convince you that I have not overrated him."

Walker's reply on 19th June was disappointing, as Wells' letter had been delayed in reaching the Englishman. He wrote that the letter had arrived at his home after he had left for the Isle of Man TT. He wrote: "I have a feeling I met him with Jim Redman when the latter was handing in his senior machine and when there was a considerable noise going on. I can recall Jim introducing me to someone whose name I didn't catch, but I have now come to the conclusion that it must have been poor Gary, who must have thought me a very odd type of man."

Walker concluded by saying that he was now writing to Reg Dearden with the list of victories John Wells had sent, and was also trying to contact Gary, wherever he was. As we will see, Hocking had more success in meeting up with Reg Dearden, and the result was a ride on the Dearden Nortons.

Wells also wrote to another of his good contacts, Gilbert Smith, MD of the Norton Motorcycle Co, so Hocking's name had been well branded even before he left the shores of Africa to return to his native UK.

To finance the move, Hocking had to sell both his 350cc and 500cc machines. According to British Airways records, his flight would have probably taken him from Bulawayo to Salisbury, then to London.

John Wells and friends saw Hocking off at Bulawayo airport with, as Wells put it, "A huge suitcase which rattled there was so little in it. His riding leathers, his helmet, affectionately known as a 'piss pot helmet' because of its shape, his toothbrush, his passport and little else."

Arthur Hocking travelled by car to London airport with Gary's younger brother Duncan and another friend to meet his son and recalled: "We met him in London and travelled down with him, and he talked motorbikes all the way. The next day," his father said, "he was up and away to the TT races. I don't think I had half an hour's talk with him since he had arrived."

Hocking met up with Reg Dearden on the Isle of Man, and also Jim Redman, who tells the story that he was about to be sponsored by Dearden himself. But as things had gone so well for him in Europe so far, and his bikes were going well, why not sponsor Gary instead? Redman was also humble enough to add "he's better than me anyway!"

Reg Dearden ran a motorcycle business in Chorlton, Manchester, and those that knew him said he was generous in sponsoring motorcycle riders, but often arrogant. He was careful with money, and earned the nickname 'Reg, dear do!' There is no doubt, according to another of his riders, that "Reg was a loveable rogue. He was a hard man for a deal, but he was good to his riders and looked after them."

Reg would look after Gary Hocking, and, having seen the letters from John Wells, he was prepared to at least give the newcomer a chance, although he did take some persuading. Things didn't look good for Sox, and he was almost ready to use the return half of his ticket back to Bulawayo, but after pouring his heart out and pleading for a chance, Hocking was eventually welcomed into the Dearden fold and allowed to see the Dearden stock, which was considerable.

The Manchester dealer would get his hands on the previous season's works Nortons, so for anyone riding them it was the next best thing to having a works ride. Hocking lodged with Dearden, and was amazed at what he saw. He wrote to Jim Redman telling him that there was just about everything you needed to build and maintain a fleet of Nortons, from frames, wheels, exhausts, leads, plugs and carburettors, right down to light bulbs. You name it, Dearden had it.

After the TT where Hocking didn't get a chance to ride the course, but having taken into consideration the letter from John Wells, the outpouring from the heart, and no doubt the recommendations from other Rhodesian riders, Dearden lent Hocking one of his 500cc Norton machines to ride in the 1958 Dutch Grand Prix – known officially as the Grand Prix of Holland – at the Van Drenth circuit.

It would be the biggest gathering Hocking would have seen in his life. Despite rain the previous day the conditions were perfect and there wasn't "... an inch of grandstand or the earth banks free," according to the *Motorcycle News* report. Hocking shared the grid with such names as Geoff Duke, John Surtees and fellow South Africans Paddy Driver and Jim Redman.

Surtees and fellow Englishman John Hartle were on MV Agustas and had been fastest in practice. They stretched away at the start of the race, but at the end of the first lap, which saw four riders crash, Hocking was third and John Love fourth. By the fifth lap he'd dropped two places, and after a third of the total distance Gary was in sixth place. Redman retired on the 14th lap, and Duke two laps later, with his bike's front brake locking up.

The crowd was enthralled by some of the racing unfolding in front of it, and you can imagine the excitement and the noise generated by over 200,000 people. At the start of the final lap right in front of the pits, the leader, Surtees, lapped Hocking and went on to win the race at an average speed of 85.7mph. He was adding the 500cc victory to his earlier 350cc win. Hocking came a very creditable sixth, thus gaining his first ever world championship point.

Needless to say there are no records of any reaction from either the winner or the novice Hocking, which today would be unthinkable. The first job of reporter at just about any sporting event is to get quotes from the participants. How did you enjoy your first world championship race Gary? What did you learn about racing at this level? Were you nervous in front of a crowd of over 200,000? How did the bike perform? Oh, to have known the answers to some of the post-race questions that are asked as a matter of course these days.

Hocking had his first European success at a small meeting in Piestany, a town in Slovakia. Small might relate only to the reputation of the competitors, as over 100,000 people witnessed the Rhodesian winning both the 350cc and 500cc races. The prize money would have been very welcome, as Sox took in the meeting on his way to the next opportunity to test his ability against some of the world's best riders, when on July 20th the circus rolled into Germany.

Reg Dearden had been so impressed with his new rider's performance in Holland that, for the race at Nürburgring, he lent him the 350cc Norton originally intended for the late Keith Campbell.

Campbell, an Australian, was his country's first motorcycling world champion when he won the 350cc title in 1957. In December of that year he had married Geoff Duke's sister-in-law, and was back in Europe for the 1958 season. He was the star rider at the 500cc Grand Prix de Cadours in France on July 13th, and was leading the race when he failed to take a bend known as Cox's Corner. The 26-year-old sustained a fractured skull, and was killed instantly.

The Nürburgring was rebuilt in the mid-1980s, but before that the track, built around the village of Nürburg in the Rhineland, contained the North Loop which was 14.16 miles in length, and had a rise of 1000 feet amongst the Eifel mountains. It was nicknamed the Green Hell due to the demands placed on the riders and the drivers (like most circuits, it was used for motorcycle and Formula One car races).

Following the Second World War, German motorsport was in confusion, and both German machines and German tracks were banned from international participation. By the time the nation was welcomed back onto the racing calendar in the early '50s, Sachsenring – Germany's main prewar race track – was in East Germany, so couldn't be used. However, in the west, the Federal Republic of Germany, there was a strong motorcycle industry being built up, including such names as NSU and DKW.

Schottenring was used in 1953, but there were safety issues and a boycott eventually ensued, so when the German Grand Prix came to the Nürburgring in 1958 it was the first time in three years. However, since that last grand prix, the track had played host to many long distance grand prix car races, and which had, in the words of one journalist, "a vicious polish on the surface and greatly worsened the bumps." Despite the condition of the track, in his book *Speed*, John Surtees described the circuit as "one of the most beautiful." Fourteen miles to the lap, 170 bends during a typical race, Surtees continues, "it is the most complicated in the world. It was difficult to remember the course, and as one bend follows another so quickly it was difficult to get into any rhythm."

The road surface had deteriorated so badly that the riders complained of bumps that made the larger bikes unmanageable. Even Gary Hocking managed to come off his Norton in practice, sustaining a black eye and cuts to his face for his troubles, and this was less than two hours before the race was due to start!

Worse was to happen for another rider, Jack Brett, but, as so often happens in sport, as a door closes for one man it opens for another, and the door was about to open for Hocking.

Englishman Jack Brett made his Norton debut in the 1947 TT riding in the 350cc and 500cc races. Apart from a spell in 1952 when he rode an AJS, Brett rode Nortons, and had been part of its works team supporting Ray Amm at one stage. Brett only ever won one grand prix race – the 1952 Swiss – although he did have 11 podium finishes from his 36 starts.

According to one newspaper report, Brett came off his machine in practice and broke both his arms. The actual accident happened as Brett was in the early stages of the 350cc race, and it meant that there was an opening in the Slazenger Norton team. Hocking was invited to take it for the 500cc challenge, and a challenge it proved to be, as the riders were not only up against their fellow competitors, but against the elements as well.

As the riders came to the grid for the start of the race, the rain, which had possibly contributed to Brett's accident, had relented, and the sun had come out. Still, though, the track was greasy and slippery, especially under the trees, which was due to the rain on the oil and rubber that had been left on the tarmac surface. Apparently the day before the race the track was crowded with people "screaming around the corners as fast as they can – or think they can," wrote one reporter, who added that the ambulances were very busy!

The two MVs of John Surtees and John Hartle shared the front row of the grid with the BMWs of Ernst Hiller and Austrian Gerold Klinger. The two Nortons of Bob Anderson and Alan Trow completed the line-up.

The two MVs screamed off at the start of the nine-lap race, chased by Hiller and Trow. Surtees soon built up a 50-yard lead. By the end of the first lap, Surtees was two lengths ahead of Hartle, with Hiller 100 yards behind, but already Gary Hocking had improved to fourth, those four pulling away from the rest of the field.

By the end of lap two Hocking on the turquoise blue Norton single had improved another place to third, and *Motorcycle News* reporter Mick Wollett was moved to write that "This Rhodesian newcomer is certainly causing a stir." As the leader Surtees began his fourth lap the rains returned, and, even though the 85,000 spectators could scamper for cover, the riders were left to the worst of the storm. The shower turned into a hailstorm and there was even a clap of thunder – needless to say, the track was once again awash. Even the press box saw the reporters moving back into dry areas.

There were probably only few occasions when Gary Hocking had ridden in rain out in Rhodesia, and certainly nothing like the torrential downpour now sweeping the Nürburgring. It must have been at the back of his mind that, sitting in the saddle of a Norton works machine for the first time, this was his big chance to impress, and he was determined to take it regardless of the weather. During the worst of the storm Hocking moved up on Hartle, before news came crackling through the PA system that he had split the works MVs to take second place: a position he held for most of the lap. This would have been about the half-distance mark when Hartle pulled down his goggles, and, as the rain lashed into his eyes and the thunderstorm unleashed its full fury, Hocking demolished the half-minute advantage the Englishman held over him.

On lap seven, though, Hartle retook second place as the sun once more came out from behind the dark grey clouds. At the beginning of the final lap, Hartle's lead over the Rhodesian Welshman was up to 13 seconds, and at the end of the nine laps Surtees won his eighth consecutive world championship with a time of 1hr 50m 51.6 sec, at an average speed of 69.92mph. Hartle was second, almost 40 seconds behind at an average of 69.48mph, but third – as the report reads in an almost live commentary fashion – "and now comes the hero of the day, young Gary Hocking." He was just over a minute behind Surtees at an average speed of 68.93mph. In his column *Paddock Gossip* in *MCN*, Mick Woollett wrote: "The circuit was so treacherous that any man who finished the 500cc race deserves a medal."

Although the MVs had come first and second, the headlines were all about Gary Hocking. "Sensation of the German Grand Prix was the riding of Rhodesian Gary Hocking," read one report. "The real hero of the German, Southern Rhodesia's bolt from the blue Gary Hocking," was another. "Hocking: future star. Hail to Gary Hocking a new rising star." The plaudits continued. In *Motor Cycling* of July 24th 1958, the clinching of the 350cc and 500cc world championship titles by John Surtees was the lead of the article, but the bulk was all in praise of the new sensation, Hocking: "... the man of the day was brilliant young Gary Hocking, the only rider who managed to stay anywhere near the MVs of Surtees and John Hartle in the 500cc race, and who actually split the well-established four-cylinder spearhead at one stage for the best part of a lap! It was an outstanding performance at any time, but one which marked this 20-year-old

Continued page 65

A race day at the Roy Hesketh circuit Pietermaritzburg, but typical of most of the South African tracks. (Billy James Collection)

Borrow Street Baths, Bulawayo. It was here that the young Gary Hocking would challenge others to see who could stay underwater the longest. Hocking invariably won. (Billy James Collection)

Typical of the type of vehicle used to transport the bikes in South Africa. Apart from carrying the bikes, these vehicles also often provided the sleeping accommodation.
(Billy James Collection)

This photograph was reproduced in a Durban newspaper back in December 1957. It is thought to be the only picture that exists of Ken Robas (middle), and Gary Hocking together, along with Jim Redman. The original has been lost, but it is worth including for its historical value alone.

Gary Hocking on Norton 38 riding to victory at Roy Hesketh in December 1957.

At Roy Hesketh again on the same machine as the previous photograph, this time number 34. Gary Hocking came fourth. (Billy James Collection)

Another early picture of Gary Hocking on the Norton.

The name 'Hocking' scratched onto the engine of the bike found by Ivor Gilson.

An early photograph of Gary Hocking on a 350cc Norton. It is thought this race could be the PE 200 Handicap event at Port Elizabeth in January 1958. (Billy James Collection)

Having persuaded Reg Dearden to sponsor him, Gary Hocking had some races against Jim Redman. Here, he chases Redman in one of their early European encounters.

Early 1958, after Gary Hocking had begun riding in Europe. Here he is on a Reg Dearden Norton chasing Jim Redman, also on a Norton.

Reg Dearden, in his familiar macintosh, applies last-minute adjustments to Gary Hocking's Norton.
(Billy James Collection)

An early ride for Gary Hocking on a Reg Dearden Norton came at Silverstone in 1959. Here, Ginger Payne leads Hocking and Frank Perris.

Final adjustments for the MZ 125 at the start of the 1959 Ulster GP.

Spectators at the Ulster Grand Prix of 1958 watch as Gary Hocking leans the 250cc MZ into a bend.

Gary Hocking on the 125cc MZ leads Mike Hailwood on his Ducati in the 1959 Ulster GP. Hailwood would go on to win the race, with Hocking second.

Apparently, the front forks of the 250cc MZs ridden by Gary Hocking in 1958 were not the same as those of the production models of that period. Note the different forks on bike number three in the background.

On the top step of the podium for the first time as an MV works rider at Censenatico, having won the 125cc race in 1960. (Courtesy Duncan Hocking)

The sun began to shine on Gary Hocking, after apparently it had rained like a waterfall for most of the 250cc race at the East German GP of 1959. It was one of the two events MV allowed Hocking to ride after he had signed for the Augusta team. Here he is on his final lap, about to win with a new record time, setting a lap record of 92.58mph (Courtesy Duncan Hocking)

Following his victory in the 250cc race at the 1959 East German GP, Gary Hocking explains to MZ race engineer Walter Kadeen and Hubert Schmidt of Radio Berlin exactly how it was done. (Courtesy Duncan Hocking)

Gary Hocking awaits the start of the 125cc race at the Italian Championships at Cesenatico, 1960. His first season as an MV works rider. The famous MV team manager, Arturo Magni, is the man to our left of Hocking. (Courtesy Agusta Museum, Samarate, Italy)

Gary with his friend and mechanic, Nobby Clarke.

On the podium having won the 1959 East German GP on the MZ. Jim Redman, also riding under the Rhodesian flag, came second, and New Zealander John Hempleman third.

The spectators get close enough to feel the wind, as Gary Hocking leans the 250cc MV into a right hander at the 1960 Spanish GP at Montjuic Park.

MV 350cc with Privat badge on the tank – post-1961.

The 500cc. The Big Red Fire Engine with the original MV badge.

Gary Hocking with 125cc and 250cc team-mate Carlo Ubbiali. To the right of the group, in the white hat, is MV team manager Nello Pagani.
(Courtesy Agusta Museum, Samarate, Italy)

Gary Hocking with Mike Hailwood, and, on the left, Ernst Degner.

Gary Hocking in the German Grand Prix on the MV 250,
with the original badge on the tank.

Bob McIntyre (3) and Gary Hocking at the 1961 Dutch TT. The two riders
rode shoulder-to-shoulder during a remarkable overtaking move from
Hocking. Count Agusta was not impressed, apparently, with the tactics.

Congratulations on another victory, from Count Domenico Agusta.
(Courtesy Agusta Museum, Samarate, Italy)

With MV team-mate, Carlo Ubbiali. (Courtesy John Wells)

Gary Hocking with Frantisek Stastny in 1961. On the left of the picture is *Motorcycle News* reporter Mick Woollett. (Courtesy John Wells)

Even though he was never much of a drinker, Gary Hocking could enjoy himself when there was time to relax. (Billy James Collection)

Gary Hocking at speed in practice for the 1959 Junior TT, where he would come 12th. Gary gave this photograph to Phil Corkill.

On the Dearden Norton at speed over Ballaugh Bridge in the 1959 Junior TT. For the Junior race in 1959, the fairing was added to the machine, whereas it wasn't fitted for practice.

The MV team would stay at the Douglas Bay Hotel, which was owned by an Italian at the time. Notice the lack of socks.
(Courtesy John Watterson)

Gary Hocking on the MV 250cc in the Lightweight TT 1960 – his first TT victory. (Courtesy Tony Breese Racing Photos IOM)

Being congratulated by runner-up Carlo Ubbiali, after winning the 250cc TT, 1960.
(Courtesy Robert Cannell)

The Rhodesian flag flies above – Gary Hocking makes the podium at the
Isle of Man TT for the first time, having won the Lightweight race in 1960.
Second was Carlo Ubbiali, and third Tarquinio Provini.
(Billy James Collection)

Mum Madge looks on as Gary Hocking takes part in his first BBC interview
following his victory in the 1960 Lightweight race. Why didn't anybody
write down the answers for posterity? (Billy James Collection)

southern Rhodesian as a rising star of the first magnitude. For not only was this just the second race he had ever ridden in the rain, but he also rode it on a machine he had never even straddled before pushing it from the line – the un-streamlined Norton, on which Jack Brett had put up the fastest practice time. Hocking had grabbed the headlines and his opportunity.

A week after making the news at the Nürburgring, Hocking took his place on the start line of the Swedish Grand Prix at the 4.5-mile Hedemora circuit. Although he had only ever ridden once before in the rain, his welcome to Europe continued to be decidedly damp. After the monsoon of Germany it rained again on practice day for the Swedish, but at least it was dry for the start of the race on Sunday 27th. It was the first time that this grand prix had been included in the world championship series, and it was rewarded with an enormous crowd.

Geoff Duke on a Dearden Norton shared the grid with Sox on a Manx for the start of the 30-lap, 135-mile race. Hocking, though, had a bad start, and the lead was taken up by Bob Anderson, who had started seventh on the grid. Duke soon pulled his race together, and was within four seconds of Anderson, with Gary Hocking involved in a thrilling scrap for third place with Dicky Dale, another newcomer Alan Shepherd, and Alan Trow.

Third place would be the best that Hocking could briefly muster during the race. Anderson's engine seized on lap 26, allowing Duke and Dale to go neck and neck over the finishing line, with Hocking eventually coming home fourth. He covered the 135 miles in 1hr 20m 10.4 seconds, at an average speed of 101.22mph

Hocking had gained a taste of world championship racing, and had proved to himself and the rest of the motorcycle world that he could compete with the best riders around. He eventually finished his first season with eight points, which had him sharing joint sixth place in the 500cc class with West German Ernst Hiller, behind champion John Surtees, John Hartle, Geoff Duke, Dicky Dale, and Derek Minter, but well ahead of fellow Rhodesian Jim Redman, who was 31st. It's worth noting that all five of the riders ahead of Hocking had the Union Jack alongside their name, such was the dominance of British motorcycling in the late '50s. Gary ended his season in England with meetings at Mallory Park and Scarborough, where he rode one of Dearden's Nortons.

Many of the Rhodesian and South African riders returned to their home country for the winter of 1958, but Hocking decided to stay in England. He was determined to learn more about the conditions, some of the circuits, and especially the Isle of Man TT, course. He spent some of the winter months on the island, where he did lap after lap on a Norton lent to him by Bob Dowty.

Dearden had an ambition for 1959, and that was to witness one of his bikes becoming the first to lap around the mountain circuit at an average of 100mph, and also to "put it over the MVs."

Hocking also spent time at Oulton Park testing a lighter version of the Manx Norton, trying out the steering and suspension. As his lap times were near to the existing 500cc records for the circuit, he declared that he was very satisfied with the setup.

Dearden was reported to be thinking of a comeback in the 250cc class, and was also interested in a fast Velocette ridden by Dave Chadwick on the circuit at Scarborough a few years previously. Apparently the Manchester man was considering experimenting with a Velocette engine and five-speed gearbox in a Manx Norton frame. He thought that, with Sox aboard, it would be a very competitive machine. You would imagine that given his engineering knowledge and skill at tuning and setting up machines, experimenting with Dearden's ideas would have made the winter pass very quickly.

Hocking now had something of a problem. He had begun to make an impact on the continental circuit; now he had to prove to the motorcycling fraternity, and to himself, that it hadn't been beginners luck or a flash in the pan. His first meaningful appointment was at Imola for an International Cup race, which had been in doubt up until a week before its April 12th start date. The Italian Federation had only then decided to run the race, but even so, it failed to keep the crowds away. There was a routine victory for Surtees despite calling in at the pits at one stage to report a bad accident involving Australian rider Harry Hinton. Despite his stop, which showed the spirit in which races were held, Surtees won with over two minutes to spare before his MV partner Hartle crossed the line. There was no luck for Hocking, as the engine on his Norton seized early in the race.

Being a young non-works rider, even though he was being supplied with bikes by Reg Dearden, Hocking still had to earn a crust to pay for his upkeep in Europe. Petrol for the van – which not only carried the bikes, but also provided sleeping accommodation – and food, which if things were bad consisted of a tin of beans, but if things were good, involved some meat to throw in as well! Therefore the chance of some prize money at a small meeting near Vienna was a worthwhile temptation and was rewarded with prize money from his wins in both the 350cc and 500cc races.

Few if any races, even the grands prix, paid more than the £200 for a win at the Isle of Man TT. If the races took place in Eastern Europe, such was the poor value of the winnings when converted back into Western currency, that the riders would often instead spend them on some of the desirable goods being produced in Eastern Europe at the time. Cameras and cut glass were some of the favourites of the time, and these were either kept by families or sold for decent money when the riders returned to the West.

If Hocking had limited experience of racing in the rain in Rhodesia, he was certainly getting all the practice necessary in Europe, as his next appointment was the Austrian Grand Prix where the weather was atrocious. It didn't worry Sox, who led the 350cc field from start to the chequered flag at the three-mile circuit near Salzburg.

There was no John Surtees to contend with in Austria, as Count Agusta had banned him from riding in anything but world championship races after a fall at Silverstone. The Count did allow one MV, though, after pleading from the organisers, and that was ridden by John Hartle. He won the 500cc event, beating Hocking into second place in a race that was scheduled to be over 20 laps, but was cut to 15 due to the conditions.

Hocking was continuing to learn, and continuing to impress, but there were concerns from some of his more experienced friends and colleagues. He still rode with the same style that he had ridden with on the dirt tracks in Rhodesia, which John Wells explained was rather like speedway riders who had one leg out on the ground at corners. "That style," he added, "followed them with their road racing overseas." Wells said that Graham Walker wrote to him expressing the view the Hocking was "pushing his luck." Wells said that he countered that by saying: "Don't worry, that is the way he rides and he will adjust himself." Later pictures of Gary at speed and leaning into corners show that he had adjusted, and could corner with that inside leg well tucked in, as all the leading riders did.

Others had also expressed concern about his riding style, saying that his career was likely to be short-lived as he was literally bouncing off the straw bales that were placed at the edge of the track. Wells countered by saying that was the way he rode – he used every inch of the track.

If anyone was worried about Sox's style or continued success, the French Grand Prix would dispel their concerns. As this race did count for world championship points, Count Agusta allowed John Surtees to ride the MV four-cylinder machine, backed up again on the 350cc by John Hartle. The pair of them by now must have been sick and tired of the sight of the Rhodesian who was like a wasp around the picnic table. Hocking set about the MVs on his standard 1957 Norton, and chased Surtees for more than half the 19 laps. Surtees admitted in his autobiography, *Speed*, that at the halfway stage he had to "open up" to throw off the challenge of Gary Hocking. By that stage the contest had been too much for Hartle's machine, which began to develop engine and rear wheel problems, and he dropped back. Only then did Gary ease up on the duel with Surtees, realising that he wasn't going to catch him, and happy to take second place just over a minute behind the reigning world champion at an average speed of 72.2mph.

There was a change to MV's team for the 500cc race, as it sent out new recruit Remo Venturi to support Surtees, whilst Hocking rode a five-year-old Manx Norton. The heavier scarlet machines were at a disadvantage to the lighter Nortons, and again Hocking split Surtees and Venturi, until a faulty gearbox on the aged Norton allowed the second MV past and Hocking had to be satisfied with third place.

It was the contest between Hocking's Nortons and the MVs that thrilled the crowd at a new track on the world championship circuit. It was the first time motorcycle racing had been held on the undulating course near Clermont-Ferrand, which contained just about every type of corner on a five-mile lap. Such was the terrain that in some places there was nothing to stop a wayward machine plunging down the mountainside, as there were no restrainers on the outside edge. Some thought that there were too many corners. Others expressed an opinion that some of the corners on the fast downhill section were too dangerous.

Surtees had only been slightly faster than Hocking during practice – or, as the *Motorcycle News* reporter liked to call it, training – but Hocking found himself in trouble before the race began. He told a reporter (you see, they did talk) that 25 laps for the 500cc machines was too long for such a tiring circuit. Having got wind of the Rhodesian's comments, the stewards insisted that he have a medical examination before he could take part. Hocking was passed fit and his position at the end earned him further praise from Surtees in *Speed*, saying "he rode a skilful race to finish third."

The first chance Gary Hocking had to try his skills on the Mountain Course on the Isle of Man came in the Junior TT in June, in which he came 12th. He was then due to ride in the Senior on a Norton, which should have been mounted by Dave Chadwick, who had rejoined the Dearden équipe but had suffered a broken arm.

As the riders and fans awoke on the morning of the race, the island was under thick cloud and steady drizzle. In places, Manannan's mantle – the mist and low cloud that forms a blanket over the mountain – visibility was down to fifty yards, and these conditions persisted all day. The organisers had no choice but to postpone the race – the only time this had happened since 1935. Many of the riders had other engagements – Hocking was scheduled to ride at Karlskoga in Sweden, and so he had to withdraw from the race listed for the following day. Another with the same dilemma was Geoff Duke, who was in the group that followed Sox home in the 350cc race in Sweden. When he won the 500cc it was another double and more prize money in what was so far a fabulous season, which would continue with another second behind Surtees in the 350cc at Hockenheim.

The FIM spring conference in 1958 had decided that 500cc bikes would be excluded from the world championships in 1960. The idea was to encourage other manufacturers to enter their machines, as only production models would be allowed. At the time that would mean Manx Nortons and Matchless G50 singles would be the favourites. So, in the interim, for the 1959 season a new series of Formula One races would be added. A machine entered in Formula One had to be the same as that sold to the general public by the manufacturer. It should be described as a Formula One model, and no optional equipment could be fitted except for safety bolts for the tyres. At least 50 units of the model in question had to have been produced and sold to the general public.

Naturally the manufacturers were against the idea, and the 350cc Formula One race at the Dutch TT did little to uphold the argument that Formula One events for production machines only would make for closer racing. The field was left to the Nortons ridden by Hocking, Redman, Bob Brown and Bob Anderson, which proved to be faster than the AJSs of Mike Hailwood and Dicky Dale.

Hocking came second, behind Australian Bob Brown. *Motorcycle News* reported that "the race lacked the glamour of other classes, and the crowd only showed lukewarm interest." Hocking failed to finish the 500cc race, his Norton suffering engine trouble on the 16th lap.

Fifth in the world championship series was the Belgian event in the pine-clad Ardennes, and again it was a familiar tale of Surtees lapping, as the *Motorcycle News* report put it, "with clockwork regularity. The only man able to approach his meteoric gyrations over the 130-mile race was young Rhodesian Gary Hocking on a Reg Dearden tuned Norton." Gary had to be content to look down the exhaust pipe of Surtees in the 500cc, but after "zooming around in wonderous style, punching the gears home as he swept through the esses," Gary Hocking won the 350cc race at an average speed of 111.07mph. "Brilliant Hocking first 350 second 500," were the newspaper headlines.

Hocking's 'brilliant' season so far had not gone unnoticed elsewhere, and in July of 1959 one report stated: "It is strongly rumoured that Gary Hocking will race MZ two strokes in the future. The East German factory is said to be preparing a mount." A week later the rumours were confirmed, and Hocking appeared in the Swedish Grand Prix at Kristianstadt on an MZ 125. The factory had prepared the machine with a gear change and brake pedal on the opposite side to normal, *ie* in the British positions, so that Sox could change from Nortons to MZs without difficulty. Hocking practised on the machine on the Saturday morning and raced in the afternoon, it being the first time he had raced with a six-speed gearbox. "I was amazed by the speed of the model, and the six-speed box was a joy to use," said Hocking, adding "If I could get a similar box for a Norton I could give the MVs a run for their money."

Unfortunately ignition troubles spoilt Hocking's debut on the MZ but the 250cc race would be a life changing experience. "21-year-old Gary Hocking made a sensational debut on a works machine by winning the 250cc at the Swedish Grand Prix," read the headline. It continued to pour praise on the performance "Riding the MZ two-stroke twin, Gary Hocking pulverised MV team-men Provini and Ubbiali who between them had won every classic 250cc race so far this year." That win and the performance, once again in pouring rain, was enough to persuade the MV team manager Nello Pagani that he had seen enough to have an unofficial chat with Hocking.

Just before going to the Ulster Grand Prix, Hocking was due to be one of the names in an all-star cast taking part in the Commonwealth race at Thruxton. He took advantage of a little time in England to visit his mentor, John Wells, who was in hospital. Despite the theory that if he beat Ubbiali and Provini in the Ulster, MV might make an official approach, he was undecided about its plans for him, as following his 'chat' with Pagani, it appeared MV only wanted him to ride the smaller machines. Sox loved to be sat on the bigger bikes, and had already proved his ability. Hocking visited Wells, whose advice he had taken in the first place to team up with Reg Dearden, to seek his counsel again. Wells, from his hospital bed, was adamant that Hocking should take the chance. "You will have your foot in the door," he told the rider. "I reckon that within the year Surtees will retire and you will be on the big machines." Once again, John Wells had given Gary Hocking some sound advice.

The seventh event in the world championship series was the Ulster at Dundrod, where Hocking, Derek Minter, and Ernst Deigner were expected to ride the small MZs up against the MVs of 'terrible twins' Carlo Ubbiali and Tarquinio Provini. In the 250cc race Hocking was expected to face stiff opposition again from Ubbiali and Provini, whom he had beaten in Sweden. There was now more open speculation that if Gary won again, there would be an approach from MV for the 1960 season. 'If you can't beat them, buy them,' was the theory that had been practised by the Gallarate factory in the past.

In the 125cc event Hocking and Degner had to be content with chasing Mike Hailwood home on his Ducati, which was his first ever world championship win. But in the 250cc Hocking set the fastest lap at 91.12mph, winning the race with Hailwood second. The major surprise, though, was that the MVs didn't turn up for the race – apparently the factory had already begun to set up the machines for the final race of the championship season at Monza three weeks later, by which time there would be a new backside on the saddle.

5

The big red fire engines

W ITH GARY HOCKING about to join the ranks of MV Agusta, it might be worthwhile taking a minor diversion here and looking at what was so special about the company and the machines. The four-cylinder machines of the MV stable not only had a great engine, but in the hands of many of the greatest riders of their time, it established an unparalleled legacy in the world of motorcycle racing. It is nice to think that one of those riders was Gary Hocking.

I do not think it is necessary here to go into great detail about the development of the engines and the bikes. We could go down the road of cylinder sizes, valve angles, suspensions and exhausts, but it probably isn't necessary. If you desire that kind of detail, I can recommend Ian Falloon's book *The Book of The MV Classic 4s*. It will suffice here to see how the company and the machine developed to lead the racing world. Few machines enjoy the legendary status of the MV 4.

The engine actually had its roots as far back as the 1930s, but the real development at Agusta came as a result of the Second World War. Under the terms of its surrender to the Allied forces, Italy was forbidden to produce any aviation products, and that included helicopters, which were the basic product of the Agusta factory. Company founder Count Giovanni Agusta died in 1927, leaving control of the business to his wife and sons. Two of those sons, Dominico and Vincenzo, formed Meccanica Verghera Agusta, to keep the company going and to keep the workforce employed. It helped that both the brothers were keen on motorcycling. The factory was in a small village called Cascina.

Their first postwar machine was a small 98cc two-stroke bike meant to provide the Italian market with a cheap form of transportation. Cars at this time were few and far between, as were the people who could afford them. Soon owners who were enthusiasts began racing these machines with considerable success, and, two years later, the 98cc had grown into a 125. A year later, 1949, the restriction on Italy producing aviation equipment was lifted, and Agusta teamed up with the Bell company and began producing helicopters again. So, the motorcycle side of the company had sound financial support.

1948 had been a fairly successful year for the 125s, and that encouraged Dominico Agusta to develop his passion for motorcycle racing. 1949, though, was a disappointment, and the Count was determined that wouldn't happen again. He recruited Piero Remor from the successful Gilera outfit. His brief was to produce a successful 125cc machine, with no requirement or interest in a production model.

In April 1950, Agusta displayed its machine at the Milan Trade Fair. It differed by having a shaft final drive instead of the chain drive of the Gilera, and an advanced suspension concept for its time. A month later, Arturo Magni (also from Gilera) joined the MV team. He has been regarded as the most significant of all motorcycle engineers, and would supervise the development of the racing bikes from 1950 until the mid-'70s. A lot has been written about the quality of the MV riders, but without Magni's genius it is doubtful whether MV would have enjoyed the racing success it did, or dominated over such a long period. At the 28th Milan Show in December, Agusta displayed a street version of the 500cc Grand Prix 4. It stole the show.

In the early 1950s, the Agusta team of riders included Les Graham, Arcisco Artesiani, Carlo Bandirola and Bruno Bertacchini. The bikes developed a little, with improved drum brakes, front forks, and wheel rims, and looked stunning in their metallic silver colours, but they were still outclassed on the international scene by the Gileras and the Nortons. They had some poor results, although they did have some success at the Italian championships and Artesiani came second at the Spanish Grand Prix with Bandirola fifth. The bikes went through a redevelopment programme for the 1952 season.

1952 proved to be a landmark year, with Cecil Standford winning the 125cc world championship title. The 500s had more success as well, mainly because Les Graham had a great deal of input into the development. According to Magni he was the best they had for putting the Agusta bikes through their tests and trials. What's more, he gained the complete respect of Count Agusta, who usually demanded control of every aspect of development. Magni said that the stories about the difficult personality of Count Agusta were true. However, none of the success of MV would have been possible without the Count's enthusiasm and his passion. He was totally committed to and involved in the racing and production bikes, but he always had to have the final word before any changes could be made. "We had to work very long hours, and every evening I would be summoned to his office to explain and justify any new development or modification," recalled Magni. One major technical difference between the MV production and racing models was the drive mechanism. The Count didn't want privateers racing against the works machines, so the racing models had a chain drive, whilst the production models had shaft drives.

Graham set about resolving the handling and reliability of the 500s. The forks, frame and engine were redesigned, but the most notable change was the use of a transversely mounted five-speed gearbox, and the chain drive on the right. Also, the machines were run on Avon tyres, used by the British manufacturers and preferred by the British riders. Initially, the changes worked. Graham was sitting second in the opening event of 1952 in Switzerland when his rear tyre started to come into contact with the mudguard; Bandirola finished third.

Graham came second in the Senior TT on the Isle of Man, but, with a little more luck, he could have won, as winner Reg Armstrong's chain broke as he crossed the line: a slightly longer race and Graham would have come first. He ended the 1952 season with a win at the Spanish Grand Prix at MV's home circuit at Monza.

For 1953, few changes were made to the machines. The major recruitment was Carlo Ubbialli to ride the 125s. Les Graham won on the 125cc at the Isle of Man TT, with MV filling five of the top six places. Then came disaster – trying to avoid two slower riders at the bottom of Bray Hill, Graham crashed at 130mph and was killed instantly.

Count Agusta was devastated by the death. Such had been the relationship between the two men, that Agusta had given over his mountain holiday home for Graham to live in. The crash was attributed to a suspension fault, and the Count ordered hundreds of tests on frames and suspensions at Monza – so many that they almost wore a groove in the track – but nothing was found. The 500s were immediately withdrawn until Monza in September.

1953 saw the introduction of a 350cc four-cylinder racer, a downsized version of the 500s. It was never conceived as a racing machine, only a training model, as 350s were virtually unknown in Italy, and in racing the class was dominated by Norton and AJS. The MV was much heavier. Les Graham had ridden the 350cc in the Junior TT just a few days before his fatal crash, but had been forced to retire due to a slipping clutch. Graham was replaced eventually by Dicky Dale and Bill Lomas to ride alongside Bandirola and Pagani.

There were further developments for the start of the 1954 season: suspension and exhaust changes, and the introduction also of a six-speed gearbox. There was the introduction of fairings, which MV was reluctant to sanction as it said they made the machine taller and heavier, and more difficult to handle. The fairings varied to suit different riders on different machines. Dicky Dale had the only world championship victory, which came at Barcelona without any fairings, as if to prove the point. He came fourth in the world championship final list, and it was a year for MV to forget in both the 350cc and 500cc classes. At the end of 1954, Dale left MV and was replaced by Rhodesian Ray Amm, who had been runner-up in the 350cc and 500cc world championships the previous year. Also, Pagani retired to take over as team manager.

Development of the machines continued apace – the engines, chassis, and controversial streamlining. A lower frame was built with a longer fuel tank, which gave the rider a lower riding position. Sadly, though, there was another disaster just around the corner for Agusta – on his MV debut, Ray Amm was killed at Imola. He was chasing the Moto Guzzi of Ken Kavanagh when he came off his machine and hit a metal fence. He was killed instantly, and not only did Agusta lose its team member, but Rhodesia lost one of its great riders, and Gary Hocking lost a hero. Amm had been one of the modern Rhodesian pioneers, who had gone to Europe and blazed a trail for others to follow.

Jim Redman sums up the dangers and deaths that threatened riders every time they sat astride a motorcycle, and the riders' attitudes towards those risks: "We became tough towards it. It was one a month, or so I thought until someone told me we lost 18 in a year. I remember driving into the gates for the Austrian Grand Prix and asking one of the riders how they had got on the previous week. 'Not bad,' he said, 'but Dicky [Dale] had a bad one.' 'How bad?' I asked, and he said 'The worst,' and I'm thinking 'There goes another one.'"

Not only did riders hear about fatal accidents, they often witnessed them as well. Redman was riding in a Dutch Grand Prix: "I was coming up on another rider, and I could see who it was by his helmet, and it was Peter Pawson, and he was taking the corner too quickly. He slid and the bike smashed him onto the road. Although I couldn't hear anything because I was on a noisy bike, I could feel the crack of the helmet on the road, and I thought 'That's him gone.' So we just kept racing on. They didn't stop the race or anything in those days because it wasn't an unusual thing. So I came around again, there is the ambulance picking him up, I come around again and there is a bloke mopping up a pool of blood. When I came in they said 'Peter's bought it today,' and I thought, 'There goes another one.' It wasn't blasé because you felt it," said Redman, "but you had to steel yourself about it and put it past you, and just hope it wasn't you next." Tommy Robinson remembers a year when 13 died, and he said, "You felt it because you knew the guys so well."

John Surtees said that he wouldn't have missed riding on the circuits as they were, adding: "I still have a great affection for a number of these circuits, despite the fact of the dangers which existed then."

Another rider thought that, as a result of the loss of life in conflicts around the world, people had become used to death – accustomed to young men being sent out on wartime missions from which they would not return – and sadly it became accepted in other walks of life as well, including dangerous occupations and sports like motorcycle racing. Death was accepted with sadness, but almost with a shrug of the shoulders as well.

Safety was nothing like it is today on the tracks. The helmets which the riders wore gave them little in the way of protection. The materials were of limited protective quality, and they sat on the top of the riders head. More modern research has shown that it is not just the top of the head which needs protection but the back, the sides and the front as well, hence a modern day helmet covers just about everything above the neck. Tracks, too, are much safer. Looking at the pictures of circuits in those days there were walls and fences right up to the sides of the racing area, a few bales of hay were just about the only protection. Today there are massive run-offs which allow any rider who comes off his machine to have ample space in which to slide before he comes into contact with anything solid.

Back at Agusta, Ray Amm was replaced by former Gilera double world champion Umberto Masetti, who made his debut in the Spanish Grand Prix at Montjuice, coming home third. That year, Geoff Duke and Gilera were dominant, but in the final grand prix at Monza, MV had its first success for the 500s. Duke was forced to retire with mechanical trouble, which left Masetti and Reg Armstrong to battle it out for first place. Count Agusta was so pleased with Masetti that he gave him a one million Lira bonus. Not actually that much when you consider the value of the Lira at the time.

The next big development came in 1956, when MV announced that it would compete in four divisions: 125, 250, 350 and 500cc. There was no problem with the smaller classes where Ubbialli and Taveri were dominating, but there was still the problem of finding adequate replacements for Graham and Amm. Many of the established riders were wary of handling the MV 4s as a result of what had happened, but 21-year-old John Surtees was building up something of a reputation on the British short course circuits on his works-supported Norton. He visited Count Agusta at Gallarate at the end of 1955, and came away with a contract to ride the 350cc and 500cc machines.

According to Arturo Magni, Surtees had an extraordinary analytical racing intelligence. He was always searching for improvements. Surtees said that there were several families involved in motorsport, such as Ferrari, Maserati, and Gilera. "It was just like the old days of duelling, but instead of doing it with guns they did it with cars and bikes." Surtees found the Count difficult to deal with and autocratic, describing him as "not the easiest of characters to get along with, a bit removed from the whole thing. To get things done was difficult because you couldn't get any changes or decisions unless you saw him, and to see him he was very well guarded. Things took time to sort out. It was a little difficult at communication." Surtees first suggestion involved a small alteration to the frame and a reduction in the amount of suspension travel.

In 1956 Surtees won at Crystal Palace and Silverstone, but in the final practice for the Isle of Man TT he collided with a cow that had strayed onto the course. He wrote off his machine, but riding a 1955 model he won the 500cc race, and, but for running out of fuel a quarter of a lap from home, would have won the 350cc as well. A red letter day came for the MV team at the Belgian Grand Prix at Spa when Ubbialli won the 125cc and 250cc races, with Surtees winning 350cc and 500. For the first time, one race team had won all four classes at a Grand Prix.

Despite falling during the German Grand Prix and suffering a broken arm, which ended his season, Surtees had become the 500cc world champion, with Ubbialli picking up the 125cc and 250cc titles – the best season yet for MV

For the 1957 season, Gilera and Moto Guzzi both withdrew their teams from racing, but due to Surtees taking longer than expected to recover from his broken arm, and a series of mechanical problems, there were no world championship rides for the MVs that year either. However, they were about to begin total domination of motorcycle racing, and enter the most fruitful period in MV history.

In 1958 John Hartle joined the team to ride the 250s, but later moved up to partner Surtees on the 500s, and without any competition from the other Italian factories they were unbeatable. They were still much heavier than the British machines, and the dominance was as much down to the riding skills of Surtees as any mechanical advantage. Surtees was again world champion in 1958, with Hartle second, and MV won all four classes in the world championships. This was the quality of the team Gary Hocking was joining, and there was pressure to show that he was worthy of the position he had been offered.

Looking back, Surtees believes that Gary Hocking justified his inclusion in the MV team. "I think he was certainly quite good enough, he was a good lad and he deserved a good ride. I didn't have any kind of social relationship with him at all, but he deserved his ride, no doubt about it. Motorcycling had a tremendous influx of Australian, New Zealand, South African, and, in Gary's case, Rhodesian riders. They were good lads, they learnt their skills coming onto the continental circus, learnt the circuits, and Gary developed well and was a good runner."

6

Joining MV

MOTORCYCLE RACING WAS having a boom time in 1959, and on the roads those who couldn't afford a car might have been able to stretch to a motorbike. Sales increased by 114 per cent. Between January and September 1959 almost 300,000 bikes were sold compared with 136,000 the previous year.

A brand new Norton 250cc twin would set you back just over £200, a Matchless 650 £277, or a Francis-Barnett 150 £110. Up against this the first mini, or Morris Mini Minor to give it its full name, was introduced by the British Motor Corporation. It would cost you just under £500 and you could stretch it's legs on the first section of the M1 which was opened between Watford and Rugby. Elsewhere on a mechanical front Christopher Cockerell's hovercraft was officially launched. On a musical theme, the well-known British pop programme *Juke Box Jury* was first shown on television in June, and Cliff Richard and the Drifters released *Living Doll*, whilst in politics Harold Macmillan won the general election to give the UK a third consecutive Conservative government: one of his new Members of Parliament was the 34-year-old Margaret Thatcher.

New inventions, new innovations, and for Gary Hocking a new adventure. MV team manager, Nello Pagani, reported the result of the discussions held at the end of the Swedish Grand Prix to Count Agusta, and Hocking's interest in signing. *Motorcycle News* of August 19th 1959 headlined the news that had been rumoured for a couple of weeks, and which signalled the realisation of a dream for the 21-year-old: "MV sign Hocking."

"Last week," the article revealed, "Gary Hocking flew to Italy, and after an interview with Count Domenico Agusta, signed a contract to ride for MV next year. The contract is for 125cc and 250cc machines, but a clause had been added that he may be called upon to ride bigger machines." That was no doubt added to ensure that Agusta got the maximum use of Hocking if required, but there was no protest from the rider, who hoped that clause would be implemented sooner rather than later. The meeting didn't go without the usual Agusta mind games – he was thought to have kept Gary waiting no fewer than two days before he saw the rider. It was worth the wait, though, as the contract was for a reported £5000.

The news even reached the editorial desk of the local newspaper in Hocking's native Newport in South Wales. "Italian firm snap up Newport rider," was the *South Wales Argus* headline. Brian Stiles' article had quotes with Gary's father, Arthur: "He is just motorcycling mad, and this contract is what he has been aiming at," he said. The article continued by giving a history of Hocking's achievements, ending by saying that "he signed the contract he has dreamed about since he first flashed across the finishing line astride a motorcycle." Hocking had impressed the Count with his second place in the 1959 250cc world championship, and his riding of the temperamental MZs.

Gary would be allowed to ride for MZ at the two remaining meetings in August in Czechoslovakia and East Germany, before making his debut on the MV at Monza. The question might well be asked at this point: having been given the works rides on the MZs, why then switch to the MV stable? Apparently the answer lies in the payment differential that the two organisations were offering. The German outfit was proposing pay on a race-by-race basis, whereas the Italians were offering the more stable guaranteed salary and more money.

As for the reason for restricting the new man to the smaller machines, it was because the Count was not in favour of riders mixing lightweight machines with the big 4s. In his opinion, it was one or the other.

As if he hadn't read or heard of the speculation that his rider was about to sign for MV, Reg Dearden still hadn't been told officially that Hocking had signed. It didn't appear that it was in the Count Agusta scheme of things to inform Dearden that he was about to poach his man. Hocking went to Dearden and told him "I've signed up for MV, Reg." Dearden wasn't one to stand in the way of a young rider's ambition. "Gary Hocking with Mike Hailwood and Dave Chadwick made a formidable team, particularly as Hocking is the best wet road rider I have ever seen. I don't blame Gary," he said, but warned that "I'm working on a couple of machines for next year's TT, and I have high hopes they will beat the MVs."

According to Nobby Clark and others, Reg Dearden idolised Gary. Ever since the likes of Jim Redman and Ray Amm had told Dearden that Hocking would be brilliant, and once the Manchester dealer had seen him ride his Nortons with style, he was hooked. "He treated Gary like a son," said Clark. There was no animosity when Sox left to join MV. Dearden appreciated that it was progress.

This would be a new experience for Hocking, who had been used to looking after his own bikes, even when riding for Reg Dearden, and he would do a great deal if not all of his own tuning. Now he had to leave that to the MV mechanics. Gradually, though, he earned their respect. He showed them how well he could ride their machines, but was prepared to ask for certain things to be done. As Hocking and the mechanics became closer, so they respected his ideas and wishes.

It looked as though Gary's skills on a wet road would be put to the test yet again on his MV debut, as the night before Monza, autumn came early to northern Italy, where it was drizzling with rain. However, on the day of the final round of the 1959 world championship series, conditions were just about perfect. Hocking was to ride the 125cc, along with old rivals, now team-mates, Carlo Ubbiali and Tarquino Provini. The MZs would be in the hands of Derek Minter and Tommy Robb. Thanks to a slip by Minter, Hocking took the lead from the drop of the flag – a lead that would last for the first lap – but all the big names were in a bunch right on his tailpipe. "Not a machine's length covers Degner, Minter, Provini, Ubbiali, Taveri, Pagani and Hocking for a dozen of the 18 laps," went the report. "Gradually, though, East German Degner began to open up a gap, and Hocking dropped back to sixth, where he finished his first works ride on an MV."

Mechanical failure ended Hocking's chances in the 250cc race – after nine laps, he coasted into the pits with a dead engine. The mechanics got the machine going again, but only for it to survive one more lap before expiring completely.

1959 had been a memorable season for 21-year-old Hocking: his first full season of grand prix racing, and he'd won his first races. He'd achieved his lifetime ambition of signing for a works team, and had gained enough points to end the season joint second with Tarquino Provini in the 250cc category, behind the champion, Carlo Ubbiali.

Unlike 1958 when Hocking stayed in Europe to learn the TT course and test machines for Reg Dearden, in 1959 he returned to Rhodesia – the first time he had been home for 18 months. He was due to take with him a works 250cc MV to race in South Africa, where he joined Bob Foster's team of tourists, but this never materialised.

He left behind speculation as to who would ride what and with whom in the MV classes. Thoughts were that, as they were planning two bikes in each class, two riders – yet to sign new contracts – John Surtees and John Hartle, would ride the biggest machines. That left Hocking, Ubbiali and another new signing, Luigi Taveri, to share the 125cc and 250cc machines. It was speculated that Ubbiali and Taveri would ride the 125s whilst Hocking and Ubbiali would team up on the 250s.

John Surtees was quoted as saying that he thought the 500cc machines were becoming too fast – something he now says was taken out of context, but the claims were supported by several of his contemporaries. Something of a surprise statement, it was followed up by him saying that if big bike racing was abandoned it would have a major effect on the motorcycle trade, and that he was wearing his cap as a dealer with a franchise in Kent.

All this was left well behind by Sox as he picked up in South Africa where he had left off 18 months previously. In the Boxing Day meeting at Grand Central, Hocking won the big Handicap race from a scratch start, and came second to Paddy Driver in the ten-lap 500cc race in which he again rode a Norton. Driver was the only rider to spoil a clean sweep for the 'tourists,' as Bob Anderson and Dicky Dale won their races as well.

On new year's day in the South African Grand Prix at East London there was a tremendous tussle between Hocking and Redman, both on Nortons, with Redman winning the 500cc race by a wheel in front of 50,000 cheering, flag-waving spectators. The meeting in East London was a huge success, and showed the interest there was in motorcycle racing in South Africa. However, the racing motorcyclist had to be a great enthusiast as machines and parts cost them a fortune. There were few new racing bikes, the trade support was little and far between, and prices of spares was sky high. A new tyre, for example, would cost in the region of £11. This might explain why Sox had a great deal of the success he had that summer on an aged, battered 499cc Norton of 1955 or '56 vintage, which had once been owned by Ken Robas. "It goes like a rocket," said Hocking, "but it has a three-inch crack in the crank, which is giving rise to some anxiety." Hocking didn't have a 350cc machine, and when John Surtees decided not to fly out to South Africa, MV decided not to send the prepared machines, even though places had been booked on the plane.

Later that month Gary became the first man to set a 100mph lap at the Sachs circuit in Bellville, scorching around the 2.97-mile circuit at 100.08mph, the ride being claimed as the greatest ever display seen at the Cape. There is a story surrounding this incident, which Nobby Clark remembered. "There was something like a hundred bottles of champagne for the first person to lap the track at 100mph. Stirling Moss was there with Chris Bristow. The motorcycles practised first and Gary did the 100mph lap and then the cars practised and Britsow did a 100mph lap. Moss said 'Hey that champagne is ours.' Gary said 'No, I did the first 100mph lap, the champagne is ours.' 'No, it's ours,' said Moss, so Gary said to Ed Fay, 'Go and get the champagne.' Well Moss against Ed Fay was no contest. So Ed went up, no one was going to fight with him because he was a big guy. Anyway, in the end they decided to share the champagne, 50 bottles each, so everyone was happy. But Gary wasn't a drinker, he might have a glass of champagne, but he wouldn't go out of his way to have a beer or anything."

The final appearance of the 'tourists' came in February at Pietermaritzburg, where Hocking, Redman and Dale all won their races. Redman's victory came with yet another story. Before the race he reported to the medical centre with cramp in his hand. The problem had been brought on by the temperature of 100° Fahrenheit, not helped by Redman's leathers. The usual remedy would have been a saline injection, but as none was available the next best thing was a glass of salty water – it worked. Although the cramp did return during the race, Redman won the thriller.

Hocking returned to Europe to face more questions about his relationship with MV, and what he would be riding in the 1960 season. He said that he still had no idea which machines he would be riding, but after Monza last season he had told the factory that he was not suited to the 125cc machine, which might have explained why it signed Taveri. He said again that he was contracted for the smaller machines, but could be called upon to ride the bigger ones. He had not heard from the factory since he had left for Rhodesia, and had no idea where his first race in the 1960 season would be.

When Gary returned to Europe, he brought with him an old friend and ally. Whist out in Rhodesia, he had met up again with his former schoolmate and fellow railway apprentice Nobby Clark. Hocking had suggested that his friend come to Europe with him, as he would be able find work. Clark accepted the offer, and the two departed for Italy. Here Clark had to be a little careful. He found the MV mechanics suspicious at first, mainly because he was a foreigner. Clark hovered around doing little jobs here and there until the Italians began to trust him to fetch and carry things. Gary, of course, trusted his friend, and included him in his travel plans. They drove the roads of Europe as they had the roads of South Africa. Clark remembers that Gary went to London and brought a car, yet another Ford Zephyr – he must have been impressed with the wreck of a model he had purchased from Happy Drapers when he was a real beginner. The MV mechanics rode in a slightly plusher fashion. They had a large van, which probably accommodated half a dozen in the cab, and the bikes were stored in the back. They drove from the factory in Italy to the racetrack in whichever country, and then returned to the factory to prepare the bikes for the next meeting.

John Surtees recalled that the teams would try to make everyone stay together in the same hotel. "They would try and get you into a hotel as close to the circuit as possible. You would make your own arrangements regarding travel, and normally for all European events you would travel by car." No more sleeping in the back of the van with the bikes now for Gary; he was living in the best hotels the teams could find in Europe.

1960 would see Hocking riding in the same team as several riders he had done battle with the previous season, now as team-mates, but unlike a team sport they wouldn't be working together during races – the competition would still be just as intense. As the season got underway the talk was about the strength of the MV team, but the politics smouldering behind the scenes at Agusta began to materialise.

March 30th, Agusta announced that MV would not be taking part in the Italian Senior championships, as the Count feared that the rivalry between Ubbiali and Provini would lead to "Something physically or psychologically being damaged before the world championship series begins."

The season began for Hocking in a series of what could be called promotional races. Clark recalls these were at minor tracks around Italy, some literally on seafront promenades. Little in the way of safety, and certainly nothing like those would take place today, but for Agusta motorcycles it was essential advertising. Prospective purchasers would be tempted by seeing what the bikes looked like, and what they looked like at speed. Soon, though, the important matters of the grand prix season were foremost in everyone's minds.

On April 6th at the Spanish Grand Prix the 125cc machine was ridden by Luigi Taveri, there was no sign of Gary Hocking, although there were no 250cc or 350cc races, so maybe that wasn't a great surprise.

A week later came news that would affect Surtees. He would not be allowed to ride his own or works MVs on British circuits before the start of the world championship season. Count Agusta would not relent on his restriction as he felt there was danger to Surtees who would be attempting to become world champion for the third successive time.

Meanwhile Hocking had been hard at work in practice with the Agusta team at Monza. He had practised on the 500cc machines, which was significant, but it was only practice. He also fell off the 250cc machine, but thankfully wasn't hurt.

Things got better for the MV team, which had success in all three classes at Cesenatico. Although the meeting was an Italian championship event, normally restricted to Italian riders, foreign entries were allowed, and two of these were John Surtees and Gary Hocking. Hocking comfortably won the 60-mile 125cc race, partly due to Ubbiala's machine suffering a seized engine, and Taveri sliding off in the pouring rain. Those conditions, of course, suited Gary down to the ground, and he ended up bringing home the only surviving MV having set the fastest lap of 71.73mph.

There was another easy win for the Agusta team in the 250cc race, this time Sox coming second to Ubbiali, and to complete the clean sweep Surtees won the 500cc race.

At the same time as Cesenatico, John Hartle, who was expected to ride the 500s with Surtees, asked to be released from the contract he had only just signed. Count Agusta had given both Hartle and Surtees verbal permission to ride their own machines in races when they were not required by MV. They would have to get written permission to race, but at the time it appeared to be acceptable. On the clear understanding that he would be allowed to ride his own machines he had brought a new 500cc Norton, but when he asked for permission to ride at Silverstone and Oulton Park he was met with a point blank refusal, even though he hadn't been included in the list of riders at Cesenatico, and wouldn't be included at Imola the following week. So Count Agusta agreed to release Hartle from his contract, and he took a parting shot at morale in the MV camp. "There is a lack of team spirit at MV and it is mainly due to the attitude of the Italian riders and some of the mechanics."

The news of course sparked the inevitable speculation about who would take Hartle's place on the spare big red machine. Mick Woolett in *Motorcycle News* asked the question: "Will the Count let Gary Hocking loose on one of the big ones? He is itching to race the 350 and 500s. If he gets one of the 'fire engines' he will be out to win. But MV may feel safer to have John Surtees and Remo Venturi.

It could be dangerous to have Surtees and Hocking fighting it out with possible consequences. The Count has a delicate problem."

The solution was revealed at Imola, when Surtees was partnered with Venturi and Masetti on the 500s. Hocking came third on his 125cc machine, but in the 250cc race his engine seized as he approached a slow corner and lost control.

Less than a month after leaving the MV team, John Hartle received a cable from Count Agusta offering him 350cc and 500cc rides on works MV four-cylinder machines in the Junior and Senior TT races. The Count had come to the conclusion that his Italian riders had no chance of winning on the Isle of Man due to their lack of knowledge of the mountain circuit. He could have offered Gary Hocking the rides, but he was anxious to avoid these two riders clashing on such a notoriously dangerous circuit. Hartle decided to accept the Agusta offer, with conditions, one of which was that the MVs he was given had to be of the latest design.

The first meeting of the 1960 world championship series came at Clermont Ferrand, and it was the end of John Surtees' two-year unbeaten run in world championship races, stretching back to Monza in 1957. "Surtees' Crown Slips" was the headline in *Motorcycle News*. "John Surtees ... was sensationally beaten into THIRD place in the French Grand Prix 350cc race. He was beaten by the dashing young Rhodesian Gary Hocking who was riding an MV. It was Sox's first outing on the 350cc having tried both a four-cylinder machine and an enlarged twin of 285cc capacity. He had decided to ride the twin and took his place on the second row of the grid. Surtees was on pole and alongside him the only machine which was likely to trouble the MVs that was a new six-speed Jawa ridden by Frantisek Stastny."

"Hocking takes a tumble – and still wins," reported *Motorcycle News*.

The win was even more remarkable considering Hocking fell off during the second lap. Having taken an early lead he was under pressure from Surtees, but, leaning into the hairpin, Sox hit one of the greasy patches and slid down the road with his machine. Surtees almost came a cropper, but just managed to avoid the sprawling rider and his bike. Hocking fired up his machine again and, to the cheers of the crowd, remounted, removed the smashed windshield, and set off after Surtees, losing just 12 seconds in the process.

The champion pulled into the pits on the 12th lap to change a dirty plug, and Hocking flashed past before the Englishman could get going again. Surtees smashed the lap record trying to get back on terms with Hocking, but ran out of race, ending up third, and beaten for the first time in 25 outings. In *Motorcycle News* column *Paddock Gossip*, Mick Woollett wrote: "Gary Hocking made his mark with MV. He was lucky to win, as not many grands prix are won by a rider who falls off and remounts." Hocking watched the 500cc race, as Surtees was back in winning form again, with team-mate Venturi in second place.

Both Hocking and John Hartle had wins at the Isle of Man TT – more of that later – but if Hocking could show how to fall off and win a race, he would now show he could overcome other adversities at the Dutch Grand Prix, which was next up. He lined up in the 250cc race alongside Ubbiali and Taveri, and as the flag went down immediately shot into the lead.

Fourteen laps were completed without much pressure being put on the leader. Then as he passed the pits the crowd leapt to its feet as Hocking's engine died, but with his usual skill and determination he fired up the machine again, disappearing into the distance. Lap 15 and there was a shock for the 40,000 spectators, as Ubialli was now leading Gary by a considerable distance. Just as modern day Formula One motor racing fans are suspicious of team tactics, so too were those at Assen in 1960. Had Hocking been told to allow Ubbiali to win the race, or had he got machine trouble? The answer came at the end of the race when Ubbiali took the chequered flag, with Gary one minute and thirty seconds behind in second place, but immediately Agusta mechanics crowded around Gary's machine – it appeared that a split pin had come out of the gear change linkage. As a result the shackle pin dropped out and it was impossible to change gear with the lever, so Hocking spent the last three laps changing gear by hand. He had to close the throttle, then push the small selector lever on the gearbox casing – normally joined to the foot change lever by the shackle pin – forward or backward depending on whether he was changing up or down.

Sox had a 15-second lead over Ubbiali at the end of 11 laps, and assuming that was about the same when his problems started, he lost an average of 20 seconds per lap over the last three circuits, despite being unable to race at full speed and the contortions he must have gone through whilst changing gear. With that result, both Ubbiali and Hocking were now level on points in the 250cc world championship standings.

In the 350cc race Gary rode the MV 4 for the first time. Despite having practised on the bigger machine, it took a few laps for him to get the feel of the bike in race conditions. He trailed Surtees, and had a real tussle with Stastny on a factory Jawa, but gradually built up a ten-second gap, which increased as the laps rolled away. Three laps to go and the pace proved too much for the Jawa, which expired, and after lapping with almost monotonous regularity, Surtees and Hocking brought the MVs home first and second.

Ten minutes after the 350cc race had ended, Gary was onto the 125cc for his final race of the day. Again, he and Ubbiali occupied the front row, and as usual Hocking got away the sharper, and increased his lead. The crowd's attention was distracted from the race as a fire started alongside the grandstand, and, watching the activities of the firemen, many of the fans missed Ubbiali overtaking Hocking at the halfway stage. Over the final seven laps the two MVs exchanged places, but there was never more than a machine's length between them. With just a few yards to go Hocking realised he was not going to get the better of his team-mate, so sat up on the bike and cruised home for a third second place of the day.

The MVs suffered something of a shock in the Belgian Grand Prix, with both Hocking and Ubbiali's machines giving the riders trouble in practice. Despite that, they both made the front row of the grid and both got off quickest. Everyone had been surprised by the speed of Ernst Degner's MZ in practice, and before the first lap had been completed, the German had overtaken Gary, who dropped further and further back as the race unfolded. He finished fifth, over a minute behind the winner Degner.

Ubbiali's win in the 250cc race gave him the lead in the world championship points total. Gary came second behind the Italian again, and there was no ride on the 350.

There were no surprises in the German Grand Prix at Solitude, viewed as one of the finest road racing circuits in the world. There was a thin international entry though, probably due to the low starting money. Subsequently there were only three races: the 250cc, 500cc, and side cars. Hocking won the 250cc by over a mile from Ubbiali, and Surtees won the 500cc event, which gave him the 500cc world championship title. The meeting was marred by the death of Bob Brown, the Australian suffering his fatal accident in practice.

Gary's final points for the season came with the second place at the Ulster behind Ubbiali on the 125, and on the same machine he picked one point for the sixth place at Monza, ending a frustrating yet satisfying season. Frustrating because on the 350cc he had the same number of wins, two, as champion John Surtees, and the same number of points, 22, thus sharing the world championship title. In the 250cc class again it was a clean sweep for the MVs, with Ubbiali being crowned champion with four wins, Gary Hocking second with two wins, and Luigi Taveri third. MV machines filled three of the first four places in the 125cc championship table, with only Ernst Degner splitting the Italian machines on his MZ. With Surtees and Venturi coming first and second in the 500cc classification, it showed the domination that MV Agusta held over the world championship scene.

So, it came as something of a shock when the motorcycle press asked the question in September 1960: "Will MV Agusta race next year?" Many Italian newspapers were carrying the story that was on everybody's lips after Monza that MV would not race in 1961. Count Agusta had said that there were so few races in Italy in which the MV works machines could compete that it wasn't worth carrying on. No matter how much publicity was gained outside Italy by winning races or his riders becoming world champions, it didn't help to sell the machines in the Italian's home market.

There was no official statement issued by Count Agusta, or the company, so Gary, John Surtees, and even the mechanics were as much in the dark as everyone else. There was only one person who knew how serious a threat this was, and that was the Count himself. He was apparently interested in the public reaction, and he may have released the story only to test public opinion and see what reaction it generated. He may well have hoped that the Italian authorities simply increased the number of events. It was a surprise announcement, as MV had built a new 125cc twin cylinder machine: a scaled-down version of the 250cc twin.

The story first hit the media on September 14th, but just a week later, despite the threat that MV wouldn't race the following year, John Surtees said that he believed that MV would continue to race in all four divisions in 1961.

As the news about the threatened withdrawal surfaced, Gary flew home to South Africa, saying that he hoped to get an MV 4 to ride in the Rhodesian and South African events. So, if he and Surtees both got machines, there could be the first Surtees versus Hocking race on the big 500s. A month later, still nothing had been fixed for the South African summer, although Hocking was still hopeful.

In November, Surtees returned from Italy still not knowing the intentions of the Count, who had been busy introducing a new helicopter at the Turin show. Everyone would have to wait until the new year, was all he could say.

Relationships between Surtees and MV were about to suffer further serious breakdown. In September, Surtees had been told that he wouldn't be required again before the turn of the year, and also that he could have machines to ride in the end of season races in England. Surtees had for some time been keen to move off bikes and into cars (something predicted by John Wells when Gary Hocking signed the contract with MV), and had arranged to drive a Lotus car in the American Grand Prix in California on November 14th. In the meantime, the Italian federation fixed the date for the Italian championships – which had been in the balance – for November 20th.

MV told Surtees he would be required, but the rider replied that there was no way he was going to give up his drive in America. Count Agusta reminded him that he was under contract until the end of 1961, and that contract could only be terminated if both parties agreed.

Whilst all this was going on, Hocking returned from Rhodesia to collect the works four-cylinder MV for the season in South Africa, and to ride in the Italian championships in Siracusa. Surtees obviously didn't turn up, and Gary won the 500cc race from Remo Venturi and Emilio Mendogni.

Before the turn of the year, it was announced that Nello Pagani would be stepping down as the MV team manager. His replacement would be Carlo Ubbiali, who it had been rumoured for some time was going to retire from racing.

Eleven days before Christmas John Surtees announced his retirement from motorcycle racing, but not necessarily to race cars instead. He wanted to make it clear that he was leaving MV on friendly terms, but added: "I have long felt that their policy of restricting the number of events that I could compete in, increased the danger of racing. It was this policy of MV which led to John Hartle leaving the team earlier this year." He went on to give a clue as to what he felt about the way Count Agusta treated his riders, adding: "In any team there has got to be a certain amount of give and take, and team members must have the opportunity of discussing differences of opinion with the boss." That statement gives us a very clear indication of the way Count Dominico Agusta controlled the business.

The Agusta brothers had a passion for motorbike racing, and they funded their passion by selling their machines – hence the need for a good race record in Italy to promote those home sales. Domenico was convinced that racing would be the best form of advertising, and they were determined to have the best team in the world at whatever financial cost. MV had threatened to withdraw from motorcycle racing once before back in 1957 – when fellow Italian teams Moto Guzzi, Mondial, and Gilera had pulled out – then decided otherwise. The rest, as they say, is history, and the fire engines went on to dominate the world championship scene.

By now Gary Hocking was something of a personality back in South Africa, and when he returned with the Bob Foster expedition for a second season he was joined by Jim Redman and Dicky Dale, with support from Peter Pawson and Paddy Driver. The crowds loved the entertainment so much, over 150,000 of them turned out between November and February. Hocking's MV 500cc was, of course, the star attraction, and in his capable hands he broke records wherever he went. Redman, too, produced the goods on his Honda, and as local Southern Rhodesians they were treated like heroes. They burnt up the tracks in Bulawayo and Salisbury, before disaster struck Hocking and his MV at the latter track, where the machine was almost written off. Factory mechanic Ezio Colombo and Hocking's skills were enough to get the precious machine back in working order, just in time to take part in the first of three meetings at Pietermaritzburg.

Gary was to prove just how good he could be on the 500cc MV. He won the 30-lap Commonwealth Invitation race, knocking chunks off the lap record. "Hocking was magnificent on a rain-soaked track," said one report. "Hocking led from start to finish as no one could live with him, and he left Dicky Dale and Jim Redman to fight it out for the minor places."

Hocking had three wins, Dale and Redman one each. That was December 11th, and as the next local races had very poor starting money Hocking gave them a miss, before making for East London on December 27th and the South African Grand Prix.

It was during this tour that Hocking was interviewed on the new Federal Television Service. This interview came after he had learnt of Surtees' retirement, so obviously the future was very much on the agenda. He was optimistic of replacing Surtees on the 500cc machines. "Although I didn't ride the 500cc MV in the world championships this year, Count Agusta has assured me that I'll ride the 'big 'uns' in 1961, and I'm confident he will keep his word. The other 350s are improving and I don't know if the MV will be fast enough."

Back in the UK, a Private Members' Bill was presented to Parliament making the wearing of crash helmets compulsory on motorcycles, scooters, and mopeds. Associated Motor Cycles' profits were soaring – £90,000 in 1959 had improved to £264,000 by 1960. Dunlop profits were up 13 per cent, and a large part of its exports went to the Middle East and Africa. *Motorcycle News'* South Africa correspondent, PEG Gibson, reported that there was a tremendous upsurge in interest in all forms of motorsport. New circuits had been started at East London and Cape Town, plus plans were being made for a new track in Durban. Pietermaritzburg Council had plans to improve and lengthen the Roy Hesketh circuit to bring it up to international standards, and to organise a TT event at the end of 1961. There were plans to offer really good start and prize money to attract the world's best riders, with the ultimate hope that one day a world championship event would be held in South Africa. After all, some of the world's best riders had come from South Africa.

All the enthusiasm manifested itself at the end of December, when 70,000 fans from all over the Union turned up for the South African Grand Prix at East London. Some of the fans camped for several days to get the best vantage points. South Africa was still running mixed meetings with both cars and bikes, and the bikes were meant to be the warm-up. Not with these stars in the saddles; they stole the show. The big names were there, and the fans wouldn't be disappointed. Hocking was on the works MV 4, and he started well until the fourth lap. Approaching Cox's Corner he had a painful fall, damaging his elbow and smashing the bike's windscreen. He lost several minutes before gathering himself, getting back on board, and setting off after Dicky Dale who was now the leader. The crowd was going ballistic, and was even more excited as Hocking started to carve his way through the field. He smashed his own lap record time after time, lifting it from 85.30mph to 88.34mph for the 2.5-mile circuit. Ultimately though, Gary couldn't catch Dale, Paddy Driver, or Jim Redman, and he had to be content with fourth place – even more remarkable when it was learnt he also lost his footrest during the fall.

So ended another remarkable and successful year for the still-young rider, who now returned to Europe in the first week of January to find out personally what the future was for MV.

7
The champion

I**T WAS JANUARY** 1961, and Gary Hocking still didn't know whether he was riding for Agusta in the coming season, or should have been looking for a new works team. One headline in the motoring press read "MV to quit racing." The article continued: "Count Agusta, the hard hitting boss of MV Agusta, has decided that there will be no works machines at the Italian championships or the world championships this season. First rumours of the withdrawal were heard back in September, but since then it appeared MV would continue as they had done since the late forties."

On Sunday 15th January, Count Agusta issued a statement in which he deplored the rise in the number of world championship events. The statement read. "For the year 1961 the Federation Internationale Motorcycliste has increased the number with a new one to be held in Argentina. This makes very fatiguing the participation in the world championships, especially for us, competing in four classes." It continued by laying blame for the state of affairs at the doorstep of the FIM, adding: "... several times the FIM has been requested to reduce to six the world championship events." It continued by suggesting that whoever had decided on the programme for 1961 hadn't taken into consideration the need for the industry to "work for the market and cannot be engaged beyond measure with sporting activity all year long. A situation like this leads us to think carefully about the opportunity to continue such a burden and therefore we have decided not to compete in the Italian or the world championships beginning with the 1961 sporting season."

The statement then went on to list the number of championships won by its riders, the number of manufacturers titles, TT wins, Italian championship wins etc, as if to let the motorcycling world know exactly what it would be missing. But then came a get-out clause: "However we do not intend to declare the withdrawal of our factory from sporting activity, because we'll continue to build powerful racing machines which we will use experimentally to improve our series production machines and to keep trained our wonderful riders." Further, it added, "... we will remain mobilized in full technical and organising efficiency to get back to racing when competitors of our category really exist and when they are able to achieve in all solo classes the results we have obtained. For Italian motorcycling sport, for our riders' sacrifices, for our own sacrifices and until other factories beat our performances, we are considering ourselves absolute champions of the motorcycling world."

It was also pointed out how much the racing side of the business was costing Count Agusta, who claimed he was spending a million lire (£600) per day.

Other factors may have had an influence on Agusta's decision. If the company decided not to race, then John Surtees would immediately be released from his contract, but he had decided to leave in any case, and Ubbiali had decided to retire from riding. MV might have found itself hard pressed without these two. This was the way Nobby Clark saw the situation as well. "Without Surtees and Ubbiali the Count may have thought it wasn't worth entering the races, but there were still several good riders under contract, including Gary Hocking and the Italian riders."

It was suggested that they would be allowed to ride the machines on a privateer basis. The first indication that perhaps the Count's decision was not as absolute as first thought came when he confirmed that the racing team would not be abandoned, but would be maintained for a possible return to racing one day. This indicated that maybe Hocking, Venturi, Mendogni, and Spaggiari may be seen on MVs occasionally. It could equally mean that they could practise at Monza, but not race there. The news may have encouraged other companies to return to racing, as they would now have a chance of winning. Agustas had grabbed 17 world championship title in the last three seasons, Ubbiali eight, Surtees seven, Sandford and Provine one each. It could have spiced up other teams like Norton, Bianchi, MZ, and Benelli in the 250cc class, and the 125cc battle could now be between MZ, Honda and Suzuki.

It could also see a return to bikes for Surtees, who, despite the withdrawal of MV, was still not going to be automatically released from his contract. Reading between the lines, his relationship with the Count had become so bad there was no way the Italian was going to let him get away easily, but he could end up riding his own machines.

Four days after the announcement from Cascina Costa, Gary still hadn't heard anything official from the factory. He said he was still hoping to ride MV 4s in the world championships, and that MV would provide transport and a mechanic or two if required. John Hartle also expressed his doubts about MV pulling out. "Don't believe MV aren't competing until they don't turn up," he said.

On 1st February, John Surtees was asked about MV's decision. "It is a bit of a surprise," he said, "but nothing they do really surprises me." Hocking received a cable in Rhodesia from MV, in effect reminding him that he was still under contract. It did not state whether he would be able to race MVs on a private basis, or whether he would be able to race Nortons this season if the MV withdrawal was complete. The MV he rode in South Africa during the summer of 1960 had to be flown back to Italy, which meant that he would not be able to ride at Pietermaritzburg on 12th February, even though he had been offered a Norton. He didn't want to risk upsetting the Count, who might take umbrage.

On 15th February there was another twist to the story. *Paddock Gossip* in *Motorcycle News* announced that "the latest rumour is that MV will race in the Italian championships, and that Gary Hocking had been offered works machines for the world championships on a private basis." The Count's threats had produced the desired effect. The Italian Federation increased the number of events in its championship from three to ten, which should have given the company plenty of opportunity to advertise its machines in its own backyard. But *The Motorcycle* magazine also suggested that pressure had been put on the Count by the Italian Federation (the FMI) with the object of keeping Italy in the world's championship picture.

The return of John Surtees wouldn't be happening. He and the Count met to 'settle up.' Having talked with his now former boss, Surtees thought that MV would race but on a reduced scale – "but don't be surprised if they turn up for the TT on the Isle of Man," he added.

A week later the whole picture changed again. "The plot thickens," read the *Motorcycle News* article. "Count Agusta has offered John Surtees works MVs for the coming season, including the Isle of Man TT. The earlier decision to stop racing seems to be waning. It seems that we will see Gary Hocking and other MV riders in some events this year, including the Isle of Man."

Hocking was practising hard at Monza on an MV 4 – probably the same machine he had ridden in South Africa. He practised as a privateer without any Agusta mechanics around, but they were present at the International Gold Cup meeting at Imola on 19th April. "Hocking wins at Imola on MV 4," was the front page headline. There was as much written about the fact that Agusta mechanics were present – one of which was Andrea Magni, brother of Arturo – as there was about the win by Hocking and the machine he was riding. "Gary Hocking won at the International Gold Cup meeting at Imola on a privately-owned MV 4," went the article, "and openly assisted by MV mechanics." Other reports suggested "A bombshell from Imola, and Gallarate mechanics were there," with pictures of a smiling Gary Hocking. The race and the appearance of MVs, even on a private basis, changed the whole picture for the 1961 world championships. Norton or AMC were expected to be the teams to beat. News from the MV factory might change that notion.

Sox rode a fine race on the Imola Autodrome, setting the fastest lap at 95.66mph, and breaking the existing lap record set by John Surtees the previous year. The large crowd watched him finish ahead of Dicky Dale and John Hartle, both on Nortons.

The next race, the first of the world championship season, was surrounded by controversy. Hocking was a last minute and hotly contested entry having taken over the entry of Frenchman Jean Touzalin. He arrived in Barcelona complete with an MV van, mechanics, and two of the MV 250s which had dominated the class in 1960. He explained the series of events. "A week before Imola I got a cable from Count Agusta asking me to fly to the factory. At that time," Hocking went on, "I didn't know what plans he had in mind; in fact, I had almost despaired of riding MVs this year. When I arrived in Gallarate I was told that I would be riding the 500 at Imola and that I would be able to do a few races this year on a private basis."

For the private competitors, the machines were given a new badge, which had large blue circles painted on each side of the petrol tank with the word 'PRIVAT' written on the circle and the MV badge in gold underneath. Hocking further explained that the machines were the 1960 models with little or no development, and entered by him, not the factory – but where Gary Hocking goes, a van and MV mechanics will follow. It looked as though Count Agusta was waiting to see how well Sox did against the other works teams, but despite any reservations he might have had, Agustas had already been entered for the West German and French Grands Prix on May 14th and 21st, and after that for the Isle of Man TT in the 125cc, 250cc and 500cc classes. Those entries were only made after the events at Imola and the fine showing by Gary, which may well have rekindled the Count's enthusiasm for racing.

The West German Grand Prix at Hockenheim was another first for motorcycle racing; the first time a world championship race was won by a Japanese machine. Kunimitsu Takahashi rode his Honda to victory in the 250cc race. The Japanese had entered a 125cc in the TT of 1959, but this was their first big marker. It proved to be the race of the day, with the 100,000 spectators thrilled by the four-way tussle between Hocking, Tarquinio Provini on a Motor Morini, and the two Honda 4s of Takashi and Jim Redman. The Honda of Redman had been fastest in practice, with Hocking fourth, but after a great start by Hocking, Redman took the lead on the first lap. The race developed amongst those four until the 15th lap, when Sox's MV began limping along firing on one cylinder and he dropped out. No such problems, though, for his 500, which had something of a walkover. After just a couple of laps he led by a mile from Paddy Driver and Mike Hailwood, with the crowd gasping at his dominance. Despite a sharp shower and some slippery patches around lap 24, Hocking won by a lap to gain his first points of the season in the 500cc class.

A week later the circus moved to France and Charade, where Gary looked certain to double the eight points for his win on the 250cc in Spain. He set a new lap record, but then his bike was again struck by mechanical trouble and spluttered to a halt, allowing his friend Top Phillis to record a 125cc and 250cc double.

Hocking did double his points on the 500, though, in what *Motorcycle News* called "a pathetic race." It was the worst entry ever for a world championship event, mainly because the organisers paid a decent price to the winners, but poor start money, which a lot of riders depended on. Jim Redman recalls that if you were a works rider, you had to go where the team wanted you; but if you were a private rider with more interest in earning money that winning championships, you would pick the races with the best start money, even if these were at the lesser tracks. This was the case at the French, and Mick Woollett in his report wrote: "As a race it was a farce and boring." After a hard 250, Hocking could take it easy going as slowly as he wanted to lead by half a mile after just one lap, and leading by a minute after ten. He eventually beat Mike Hailwood by a minute and 20 seconds.

If the French had been 'boring,' the Dutch TT was a thriller – in fact it was described thus: "The 350 race was as thrilling as any ever witnessed by a road racing crowd." In a fantastic duel with Bob McIntyre, Hocking proved that he was certainly in the same class as John Surtees. On the last lap McIntyre was 30 yards ahead of Hocking, and around the back of the course that was increased to fifty yards. The crowd of 150,000 was enthralled as it watched a fantastic piece of riding by Hocking who, on one of the most acute bends on the 4.5-mile circuit, left his braking fantastically late and took 50 yards off the Scot, closing the gap and forcing his way into the lead. McIntyre pulled level again, and the machines almost touched as Hocking refused to give way and the Scot was forced to close the throttle. No praise was too high for Gary Hocking's performance, as few people got the better of Bob McIntyre when he was mounted on a faster Bianchi machine.

"The last lap was just about as breathtaking as I've ever seen," wrote Mick Woollett. "We can look forward to several more Bob McIntyre versus Gary Hocking dices before the end of the season."

Count Agusta, though, wasn't best pleased at Hocking's tactics – in fact, it was said he was infuriated. He was proving to be a worthy successor to Surtees, but his relationship with Count Agusta was always uneasy.

So Hocking had his first win in the 350cc world championship title race, giving him 14 points. His win on the 500cc when only Mike Hailwood managed to stay even close to Hocking, gave him 24 points – a point better than Hailwood.

Hocking wasn't satisfied with his win at Assen, and returned to the Agusta factory on a mission to persuade the bosses to build improved streamlining. He had seen that McIntyre's Bianchi had been faster over a straight line than his MV, and thought that this would solve the problem. They obliged with a slimmer, more businesslike product, which did indeed make the 350cc go faster. He kept the bulbous fairing on the 500, and when asked why, replied: "I had enough trouble persuading them to make one, I dare not ask for another."

Different tyres were used at the Belgian Grand Prix at Francorchamps, which helped the leading riders attain faster lap times. The tyres apparently helped with cornering. Francorchamps was one of the most famous and spectacular courses in the world, and a place where speed was the keynote. There were ultra fast curves and long straights with bends being taken at 140mph. The only slow spot on the whole 8.76 miles was La Source, the hairpin. It was a place where skills and nerve were needed in abundance, and Gary showed he had both by putting together the fastest lap in practice, no doubt aware that there was now a mounting challenge from Mike Hailwood. Hocking shared the front row for the start of the 500cc race, with the four Nortons of Hailwood, Phil Read, John Hartle, and Paddy Driver, plus Ron Langston's Matchless. It turned into a one-horse race with Hocking half a mile ahead of Hartle after two laps which increased to a full minute by lap eight. Eventually Sox completed the 15 laps over two minutes ahead of Hailwood, having set the fastest lap of 4 minutes 15 seconds at 123.48mph, beating Surtees' record of 122.60mph.

Hocking's fourth win gave him 32 points in the championship title race, with Hailwood four behind as they moved on to the East German, where again history was being made. This was to be the first world championship motorcycle road race held behind the iron curtain. Over a quarter of a million spectators descended on the Sachsenring circuit, where they had even erected temporary stands. There was a sea of faces in every direction, with people marching to and fro like ants . The 5.2-mile circuit had been re-surfaced since the previous German Grand Prix's had been held on the track, a stipulation laid down by the Fédération Internationale de Motocyclisme to bring it up to world championship standard. It was worth the effort as with the spectator entry fee of three marks, plus grandstand charge, car park and programmes, the event netted over a million marks.

The 350cc race promised to be the most exciting, as both Gary and Frantisek Stastny set new lap records in practice: 3 minutes 31.4 seconds for Hocking, 3 minutes 31.8 seconds for the Czechoslovakian. Records were smashed in the race itself, before Hocking wore down Stastny and the event "settled into a procession and became dull," according to one report. Sox was over a minute quicker than Stastny and third-placed Bob McIntyre, lapping at over 1mph quicker.

There were few problems for Gary in the 500cc race as the MV 4 gave it's pilot a major advantage at the start, and the race settled into the usual pattern of the Agusta leading with the rest chasing. In this case the chasing pack was led by Hailwood, but he couldn't get to within a minute and a quarter of the winner. The crowd went crazy and flooded onto the track when Hocking crossed the line for his fifth win in the 500cc class. He now had 22 points in the 350cc class and 40 points in the 500, where the world championship title was now within touching distance.

12th of August 1961 at Dundrod in Ireland was to prove to be the day when Gary Hocking achieved his ambition of becoming world champion. In the first two races of the day, the 125cc and 250s whipped the crowd into "a frenzied melee," according to *The Motorcycle* of 17th August 1961. To match that, it was anticipated that the 350cc race would have to be "a humdinger" when Hocking had a chance to gain more points; only bad luck could stop him becoming champion in this class as well. The report suggested that "Gary Hocking certainly tried to oblige," and he showed in this race the form that he was in. From a standing start he covered the first lap at 89.3mph, the first full lap at 124.2mph, and the second at 130.7mph. Hocking had a 3.5-second lead over Bob McIntyre on the first lap, and increased that by something approaching three seconds per lap. He had a 15-second lead over Bob McIntyre when the Scot was forced out of the race at Ireland's Corner with a broken layshaft on lap seven. By halfway, his lead over Alastair King was 47 seconds, and with the MV purring along, Sox could take it easy. He covered the 20 laps – 120 miles – 1 minute 20 seconds faster than King, with Stansty third.

The champion would be crowned without a doubt if Hocking won the 500cc race, and he set out to prove that he would be a worthy master. No 'safety first and just finish amongst the points' here – he was out to win, and win in style. The only problem would be the weather. The first spots of rain fell as the riders set off. Two riders, Ellis Boyce and Hugh Anderson collided just a couple of yards from the start, but there was a worse accident on the second lap. As the roads became more slippery, Tom Phillis crashed out of the race at the Quarry and, trying to avoid Phillis, Roy Ingram came off as well. Tragically one of the machines hit a flag marshal named as Charles Walters, who died on his way to hospital.

Despite the worsening conditions, Hocking's ride was described as "fantastic," and he was soon out of sight from the rest of the field. Three laps were covered with speeds up to 139.5mph and already a lead of 41 seconds over John Hartle, who was forced out with mechanical trouble on lap five. The lead then was up to 73 seconds over second place Alastair King, and by lap 12, as long as the MV kept going – and it didn't need to be pushed – the race was virtually over. That was shown in the time and speed at which Hocking won. His fastest lap was 98.37mph, and the average speed only 90.49mph, but such was his dominance he lapped all but three riders, winning by a clear two minutes. He almost had time to celebrate becoming world 500cc champion before the second rider, Mike Hailwood, crossed the line – not that Hocking was one to really 'hit the bottle' and celebrate.

Nobby Clark recalls that Gary was delighted to have won the race and become world champion; the first Rhodesian to hold that title. He called it subdued excitement, but to Sox it was just a case of that's done and dusted, now let's get ready for the next race. Clark doesn't think that Gary got the credit he was due, and to be honest it is a feeling I share, which prompted this record of his achievement. Clark recalls there were plenty of congratulations from Rhodesia – he even received a personal message from the president, Sir Roy Welensky.

Paddock Gossip in *Motorcycle News* congratulated Gary on becoming world champion, and followed it up with news that fans at Mallory Park in September would have the chance to see the new world champion in action on his MV 4. But almost before the celebrations had died down, there were storm clouds gathering.

Almost as Hocking crossed the line in the Ulster Grand Prix, rumours were circulating that Mike Hailwood might be on an MV 4 as early as Monza, which was on 3rd September. Later in August, rumours from Italy and England increased the speculation. Hailwood's team would not confirm or deny the rumours, but it was well known by now that the Hailwood 'team' was trying to persuade Count Agusta to loan or sponsor a pair of 4s. But who was doing the persuading is a matter of conjecture. One theory is that Mike's father, Stan, was the one dealing with the Count.

Stan had been a motorcycle racer since the 1930s, and ironically enough, raced against John Surtees' father, Jack. Stan was seldom beaten. He had been hired as a mechanic by Howard King, who opened a motorcycle franchise in Oxford. Hailwood senior became sales manager, and eventually took over the company as managing director. From one branch, Hailwood turned the company into a nationwide organisation selling motorbikes in large numbers. That, it is thought, was the carrot he dangled in front of the Count. There are stories that Mike was less than impressed with his father 'pushing' his career, but it is suggested that Stan offered the Count the opportunity to sell large numbers of MVs in his shops if he gave his son a contract.

Whatever the rumours and conspiracy theories, there was no doubt that the negotiations were taking place, whichever form they took. There came a more definite turn when Hailwood, who had been racing at Aberdare, dashed away from the South Wales track to catch a flight to Italy with Bill Webster. Webster had been acting as negotiator for Hailwood, and there had been quite an amount of correspondence between him and the Count, who were old friends.

Thoughts of Hailwood had to be put to one side as Hocking prepared for the Race of The Year at Mallory Park: an event worth no less than £1000 to the winner. He took advantage of an offer to get some practice time from the course owner, Clive Wormleighton, as he hadn't raced there since 1959, when he'd been riding one of Reg Dearden's Nortons.

Whilst practising at Mallory, Hocking was asked about next season. "I hope to defend my title and although Count Agusta hasn't said anything definite, I am optimistic about my chances of riding the MV 4s again," he said. As the negotiations between Agusta and Hailwood continued it must have been an anxious time for the new world champion, as his contract with MV was due to expire at the end of the calendar year, and if Hailwood was taken on it could mean that Hocking's contract wouldn't be renewed.

The meeting didn't go without Count Agusta emphasising exactly who was in charge of the negotiations, as Hailwood's party was kept waiting and waiting – so much so that Mike was ready to call a halt to the entire proceedings. Presumably, he felt that if the Count was prepared to keep them waiting as long as he had, then he wasn't worth dealing with, despite the prize at the end of it. As Hailwood was preparing to leave the office, as if realising that he had pushed them far enough, the Count emerged, welcomed them into his domain, and an agreement was reached that Hailwood could practise at Monza to get the feel of the 4s, and so prepare him for the Italian Grand Prix.

Gary Hocking was already 500cc champion following his success at Ulster, and was virtually certain to be 350cc champion as well following his three wins, and his second at the Isle of Man. The Italian Grand Prix on MV's home track would provide extra needle, though, as lining up alongside him was Hailwood – also now on an MV. The result would be a foregone conclusion in the race for the championship, but to Hocking and Hailwood it was the start of a sometimes bitter rivalry. The gauntlet was thrown down in practice, with Hailwood setting the fastest time, and Hocking close behind.

As the race started, Hailwood led off and built a 20-yard lead. Hocking dropped to third when Brambilla, on his Bianchi, overtook him. The crowd was loving it. By the tenth lap things were back to normal, as Hocking had overtaken Brambilla and Hailwood; in fact, Sox now had a 200-yard lead over Hailwood, but he wasn't for giving up. So-called experts had said that Hailwood hadn't had enough practise time on the MV 4s to mount a serious challenge, but he was to prove them wrong and provide the champion apparent with something of a shock. The crowd was on its feet as the Englishman fought back again, and by the end of the 27 laps, just over 96 miles, just six seconds separated the leader, Hocking, and Hailwood. The win confirmed 23-year-old Gary Hocking as double world champion at 350cc and 500cc, but what must have been equally satisfying to Sox was that he had beaten Hailwood.

Gary would have been more than keen to give Hailwood another lesson on who would be boss in the MV camp, in the 500cc race. In practice he had returned a time two seconds faster than that of Hailwood, and he got away faster at the start. Both riders had spells in the lead, but, by lap 11, Hailwood had a 100-yard advantage. That had been given up to Hocking by lap 18, but, pushing his bike too much, Hocking lost the 4 with four laps to go, and gave Hailwood an easy trot to the chequered flag. It was the first time in four 500cc races that Sox hadn't won. He put that record straight in the Swedish Grand Prix at Kristianstad, when he was back to winning form on the 500. He had to retire in the 350cc race with magneto trouble: ironic, as the following week's *Motorcycle News* carried an advert for Lucas magnetos, using Hocking's recent wins and his world championship as an example of the product's reliability!

Following the Italian Grand Prix it was confirmed that Mike Hailwood would be riding 350cc and 500cc machines for MV in 1962. There was no news about a contract for the new world champion – *Paddock Gossip* in *MCN* reported that "after a year of being MV's main rider, Gary Hocking is not best pleased that Mike Hailwood has joined MV, but is still optimistic about his chances of getting works MVs for 1962. He thinks the Count will make machines available for both of them."

So, with MV uninterested in spending the necessary time or money to take part in the final world championship meeting of the series in Argentina, Sox had one last race to prepare for before returning home to Rhodesia. The Mallory Park International meeting in September would see him come up against Mike Hailwood once more, but this time, as his contract with MV hadn't started, Hailwood would be riding a Norton.

60,000 spectators came to the Leicestershire track, causing mile-long traffic jams on the approaches. Hocking would ride an MV with a 500cc engine in a 350cc frame, which would also carry improved streamlining that Gary, in sizzling form, carried to victory.

Quoted in an article from an unknown publication, titled *On The Road With John Surtees*, the former world champion wrote: "Gary has ridden extremely well this year, although in obtaining the 500cc championship I feel he took greater risks than were really necessary by driving the machine too near the limit. He is a very self-confident rider; indeed, the only thing likely to stop him is the over-confidence of which he is sometimes guilty."

And so the season in Europe came to an end, and it was time to return for the South African one. Hocking would be named Rhodesian Sportsman of the Year for the second time, having already received the award in 1959. He had hoped, as world champion, to take the now famous MV with him, but Agusta decided that there were not any bikes available, which left the local hero without a machine to ride.

Gary could have been left kicking his heels, and there are a couple of theories as to what really happened next. John Wells believes that Hocking was leant an AJS 7R by a friend, Bruce Beal. This is supported by the report in *Motorcycle News* that Hocking opened the season on a borrowed AJS 7R. Shaun Robinson, however, doesn't agree, believing that if Hocking did borrow a 7R, it was only for the first race as he awaited delivery of his own machine from Plumstead. Phil Read, who rode in that South African series, also said that Gary had his own machine.

The 7R was in such great demand that AJS would send one to a lucky dealer in, say, Manchester, another to a dealer in London, and a single machine to other fortunate dealers here and there. But such was the interest in motorcycling in South Africa that no fewer than six were sent out to Bulawayo, and through the Van Rooyen's garage and its association with the AJS factory in Woolwich, Hocking got his hands on one, with Beal getting another. It was for this machine that Gary made the fairing, which was apparently beaten out of a sheet of metal on an old tree stump, before being cast in fibreglass.

Between them, Hocking and Beal tuned their machines to perfection, and there are valid claims that these were the fastest AJS 7Rs anywhere in the world at the time. Phil Read agreed that Gary and Beal worked on their machines, and they were like lightning. Most of the bikes at this time in Rhodesia were fuelled by nitro, and this was confirmed by Read having a crafty look into the carburettor on Gary's. He was caught by Sox, and the two fell out for a little while. Nitro was a very high octane fuel, which made the bikes go faster, especially after Gary's tuning, but the pistons, cylinder head and combustion chamber would require a great deal of modification. The fuel was later banned, especially as it became so expensive to buy.

Robinson thinks that Hocking wanted it known that he was riding a 'borrowed bike' so that he didn't upset MV. Robinson knows that Gary sold his 7R to his brother, Tommy Robinson, before he returned to Europe at the end of the South African series.

The season began with a meeting at Zwartkop near Pretoria, where a record crowd of 10,000 turned out at this small track to see their latest hero. The report sent back to England for *Motorcycle News* informed the readers that Gary was the star of the meeting, and in a class of his own in the 350cc race, where he romped away from the drop of the flag.

There was no Surtees and no Hailwood to add spice to the series out in South Africa, but Hocking had duel after duel with another up-and-coming Englishman, Phil Read. Riding the borrowed AJS, Gary came third in the 500cc race at Zwartkop behind Read and Paddy Driver.

A week later, the season opened in Rhodesia with more record crowds packing into Kumalo. They were kept on their toes according to the reports, as Hocking, Read, Jim Redman, and Paddy Driver fought out a high-speed race over seven of the ten laps. With three laps remaining, though, Sox piled on the pressure and pulled away beating Redman to the line. It appears that much of the race had been run with the tactic in mind which Redman has described earlier in the book. For the sake of safety, the riders would dice with each other over the early laps to entertain the crowd then race to the line. Accidents were less likely to happen over three laps than over ten. Phil Read confirmed that they would run the race in this fashion, giving the crowd entertainment as first one rider then another would take the lead, but the riders would only 'race' over the final couple of laps.

The climax of the day at Kumalo came in the Star Riders Handicap. Despite the heat wave that had baked everyone earlier in the day, as the riders went to the grid rain began to fall, making the track surface slippery. This would play into the hands of the experienced riders and especially Gary who romped through the field to win on his AJS beating Phil Read on his Matchless and Redman's Norton.

Following Gary's world championship title and the current riders from South Africa, Mick Woollett wrote in his *Paddock Gossip* column in *Motorcycle News* of

December 6th 1961, that he could see no reason why South Africa couldn't be granted a Grand Prix meeting. Apart from the riders, serious attempts were being made to build better circuits, and judging by the crowds which were turning out to watch the latest series of races, a Grand Prix even would be well supported. As a rider Phil Read confirmed Woollett's point of view. The support out there was huge and the tracks were getting better, especially at Westmead.

The next races were held at the newly improved Roy Hesketh circuit at Pietermaritzburg. The Zulus called it 'the place of elephants,' and it was a place to forget for Phil Read who crashed during the Dicky Dale International Memorial race and missed the big race later in the day. Gary brought the 7R home in front of Ian Burne and Shaun Robinson in the Handicap event, and he also won the 350cc race after a terrific scrap with Driver, Redman and Tommy Robinson who frustratingly ran out of fuel on the last lap. Hocking won by a minute from Driver who had his revenge in the 500cc race. Driver, Hocking, and Redman again had a terrific scrap before Redman was forced to retire with a broken tank strap. But on the last of the 30, Driver just managed to keep his Norton ahead of Hocking to take the chequered flag.

By the week before Christmas, Read had recovered from his spill at the Roy Hesketh to take his place at the start of the races at another track that had seen vast improvements: Westmead. Over £90,000 had been spent on the circuit which now included an iconic tyre bridge over the start and finish line, and a control tower made of brick!

The estimated opening day attendance was 60,000, who witnessed what was now becoming the norm. According to the reports, Hocking 'walked' the 350cc race at an average speed of 82.70mph, with Driver ahead of Read, who came home third. There was frustration, though, for the crowd, which saw second-placed Hocking pull up when the engine on the 7R failed on the 20th of the 22 laps of the 500cc race.

The most important meeting of the series took place on Boxing Day at East London, where Read was back to his best form. He not only won the 500cc race, but also took his G50 Matchless around the track lifting Gary's lap record from the previous year of 84.97mph to 85.73. He won the event from Paddy Driver's Norton, with Gary a few seconds behind in third. In the 350cc race, though, Gary was in great form, winning from Driver, with Read third.

The final meeting of the South African series, due to take place at Roy Hesketh, was cancelled – the reason isn't known, although one theory is that the start money was so low that riders withdrew in numbers, making the event less than worthwhile. Money must have been good that summer, however, as Read recalls he won enough to fly back to Britain and buy a secondhand Jaguar with his winnings.

Read, Redman, Driver, and Gary all shared a house in South Africa, and Phil Read got to know Gary very well. He found him a little aloof from the others – that isn't to say he was rude or unfriendly, but he was aware that his number one priority was motorbike racing, and socialising came a distant second. He would often be tinkering with his machine whilst the others were out celebrating.

So ended the South African series, but the return to Europe for Hocking would not be without its problems. He asked Count Agusta to pay his airfare back to Italy, but the Count not surprisingly refused. Reports from Italy suggested that Agusta was angry with Hocking, whom he accused of breaking his contract with MV by riding the AJS in South Africa. "Where is Gary Hocking?" asked *Motorcycle News* when the season began in Modena. Hocking would return, and would be back in time to renew his acquaintance with the Mountain Circuit on the Isle of Man.

8

Isle of Man TT

A LL SPORTS HAVE their Blue-Riband events and venues. Speak to a tennis player, and the one they want to win is Wimbledon. Mention football, and an Englishman thinks of Wembley, an American the Super Bowl. For many years, the Mecca for a motorcyclist was the Isle of Man; and some would say it still is. Someone synonymous with the island and its TT races is Geoff Duke, who once suggested that winning a TT was bigger than winning the world championship, to which, up until 1976, it was a contributor.

John Surtees rode and won TT races, and he believed that in the '50s and '60s it was the biggest challenge to be conquered. The best riders came, and for a couple of weeks the Isle of Man grabbed the attention of the motorcycling world. Phil Read was another who rode the famous circuit in the Hocking era; he called it the "greatest challenge to man and machine."

In 1904, the Automobile Club of Great Britain was looking for a venue to stage a car race as an eliminator for the Gordon Bennett Cup, a one-time major competition in Germany. As mainland Britain had a blanket 20mph speed limit, and the authorities were unwilling to close any roads for the event, the Isle of Man seized the opportunity.

A law had to be passed in the island's parliament permitting the roads to be closed, and that law is still in situ today, allowing the present races to take place. Fewer than a dozen cars took part in the trials, but the event attracted a large crowd. A year later, motorcycles joined the cars when the Auto Cycle Union used the course as an eliminator for the International Cup to be held in France.

Seven bikes took part in the race, which was held in the south of the island: only two finished, but history had been made, as the magazine *Motorcycle* pointed out that these were "The first legalised road races for motorcycles ever staged."

It appeared that a certain amount of ungentlemanly conduct was taking place, in that foreign riders were fitting engines that were far too powerful to suit the

Spartan frames of the current bikes. A conversation took place between Henry Collier, who later went on to found the Matchless company; Freddie Straight, secretary of the Auto Cycle Union; and a French nobleman, Marquis de Mouzilly, also a committee member of the ACU.

Their conversation centred on the possibility of a competition for touring machines. There would be limits on engine size, petrol consumption, and speed, thus developing an 'ordinary touring machine.' This followed the development project that cars had taken in previous years, when they raced for a Tourist Trophy on the Isle of Man. The Marquis, not being short of a bob or two, offered to put up a 'Tourist Trophy,' and provided a magnificent prize of Mercury standing on a bike wheel with wings, all mounted on an impressive stand. The trophy was commissioned; all that was needed now was a race to win it.

The first rules were laid down in 1907, which stated that bikes should be of the touring type, have a saddle, brakes, mudguards, an efficient silencer, a two-gallon fuel tank, and at least five pounds of tools in a tool box! The engine size was not to be more than 500cc, but pedal power was an option. There were also rules as to how the race was to be started: pedalling was allowed, but warm-ups were forbidden. The size of the fuel tank was later reduced to a gallon and a quarter, which meant that there would have to be stops to re-fuel over the ten-lap course.

The course set off from Tynwald Hill, traditional home of the Manx parliament, headed north to Kirk Michael, before turning south along the west coast to Peel, and then east back towards Douglas. The road surfaces were atrocious, loose, rutted and dusty, and hedges overhung the narrow lanes. Even so these early champions attained speeds of 60mph.

As in the modern day TT, the riders set off in pairs, Jack Marshall and Frank Hulbert, the first competitors to ever tackle an Isle of Man course, both rode Triumph machines. Riders had to take a 'lunch break,' but eventually after struggling around the course and all its obstacles. Charlie Collier became the first ever Isle of Man TT winner.

The race has gone through numerous changes and developments since those early pioneers, including a change of course in 1911 when the mountain came into the story, which would add a different challenge to man and machine. However, this story is not so much about the race, but about one competitor: Gary Hocking.

Having taken the advice of John Wells to come to Europe, and having decided that whatever riders like Jim Redman could do, Gary Hocking could do better, Sox arrived on the island just in time for the 1958 races, but of course too late to enter. He had a letter of introduction to Reg Dearden, and another introducing him to Graham Walker, but he had to be content with watching John Surtees clean up in the 500cc and 350cc classes, Tarquino Provini win the 250, and fellow Italian Carlo Ubbiali winning the 125cc race, all on MV Agustas. Hocking must have been frustrated kicking his heels around the paddock, and watching the races from the grandstand area. At least he had the opportunity to talk to competitors, maybe pick up a few tips here and there, and perhaps even have a dabble at tuning some of the non-works machines. Whatever, Hocking got a taste of European races, and a chance to mingle with some of the big names in the sport.

As we have already seen in an earlier chapter, the letters to Dearden and Walker had a mixed reception, Walker thought he had met Gary, but because of a hearing difficulty may have missed his name when they were introduced. As for Dearden, with the recommendations from the likes of Redman, Castellani, Paddy Driver and others, the Manchester promoter was prepared to at least have a look at this youngster.

After the 'Continental Circus' moved on from the Isle of Man, Hocking got his chance in the Dutch, German and Swedish Grands Prix, but when the South Africans returned for a summer season back home, Hocking decided his time was better spent preparing for the race everyone wanted to win: the Isle of Man TT.

Reg Dearden sent him over to the island to learn from two local riders, George Costain and the late Bob Dowty, whom Dearden knew and trusted. The island lives for the motorcycle races, the TT being the biggest, but it also hosts the Manx Grand Prix over the same course, and the Southern 100, run as its name suggests in the south of the island.

Both riders had been regular mounts on Dearden Nortons, but Dowty was surprised to get a call from the Manchester dealer asking him to show a young up-and-coming rider around the TT course. "Reg phoned me up and said that a guy he was trying to support by the name of Gary Hocking, was going to be on the island, and would I give him a run around the TT course? Obviously I was delighted to do so, but I was a bit hesitant to take him because he was a much better rider than I was, he was a professional rider. I was happy to take him out, but explained to him before we started that I wasn't going to tell him how to take any particular corner, but all I could do was show him the course and give him some tips on the best way to learn the course, because it is 37.75 miles long, and has numerous corners of all sorts of shapes and sizes, and it does take a bit of remembering.

"Gary was happy to go along with this, he was a taciturn chap, he didn't say very much and I wasn't sure whether he was just bored with what I was telling him or whether he was taking it in, but knowing Gary and his future success I think he took a lot of it in." Dowty added that to really get to know the course, it was no good driving or riding around time after time – the best way was to learn the course section by section. Also, it was advisable to follow the example of people like Geoff Duke, who used to get out of his car and walk three or four miles looking at every bend and such things as the road surface. "The only other advice I could give him," continued Dowty, "was to always remember the blind bends where you don't have to shut off, as this will save you a lot of time."

Dowty was quick to point out that Gary's success was not down to what he had told him, as anyone who had taken him around the course would have given similar advice.

George Costain received a similar telephone call from Dearden, asking if he could help the young Hocking. Costain doesn't know if the idea of Sox coming to the island was Gary's idea or Reg Dearden's, but certainly Dearden had never sent anyone before or after to learn the TT course. "Reg had done me a lot of favours so I did Reg a favour. Gary didn't know who I was, so it must have been Reg's idea for him to stay with us." Dearden provided a road bike for Hocking to ride around the course, which he did, time after time, but no-doubt also taking Bob Dowty's advice to walk sections as well. George Costain recalls that even though they tried to make his life on the island a pleasant one, they could do nothing about the January weather. "I called him 'Taffy' because I knew his background, but he never said whether he felt Welsh or Rhodesian. Poor lad, it was so cold he spent most of his time sat on the fire to try and get warm!"

Bob Dowty only spoke to Gary on the one occasion when he showed him around the course. Bob was always too busy minding his business to spend time up on the TT course, but he did have the chance to watch Hocking ride on one or two occasions. He says that he suited the event. "Not only his style but his stature and his build as well. He was jockey type, he wasn't over weight and he wasn't over tall, and that is a big advantage. The taller you are the more difficult is it is tuck yourself in and get streamlining, but Gary could tuck himself in even on the smaller bikes. He was physically strong, and yes he was ideal."

Bob lent Gary a Norton Dominator and he did several laps of the course. *The Isle of Man Examiner* carried a picture of Hocking on the bike, well wrapped up against the cold. It said how he had been well received by the members of the Manx motorcycle fraternity, who had given the Southern Rhodesian a warm welcome. Hocking admitted to some confusion on his first solo lap – shared with the general traffic, he turned off the course at Cronk-ny-Mona, and had to do a quick reverse to rejoin the course.

A week after his trip to the island, Hocking was interviewed, along with Reg Dearden, on the television programme *Sportsview*. Questioned by a Gerry Loftus, Hocking agreed that the TT course was a real testing ground for rider and machine.

Having spent time on the island and learnt the course as best he could without the white heat of competition, Hocking was ready for his first TT race in 1959. The weather for practice was almost perfect. Such was the interest and importance of the annual event, a special newspaper was printed, *The TT Special*, and it tells us that: "Never before, so long as we can remember – and our memory is a long one – has there been such perfect weather for TT practising. On each day apart from the last one conditions were ideal. There was a light mist on the mountain this morning [the final Saturday]." There had been few accidents, certainly none with life-threatening consequences, which was something of a surprise to the editor of the paper, GS Davidson, as there were 50 newcomers to the TT that year. One of those, of course, was Hocking, who would be riding one of 16 Nortons sponsored by Reg Dearden.

John Surtees produced the first 100mph lap in that year's practice on the 500cc MV. Surtees had already achieved a 100mph lap in the races of the previous year.

The first practice session on Saturday 23rd May took place on a perfect evening. The scene was described in *The Isle Of Man Examiner*: "As the Fleetwood boat sails into the sparklingly calm sea and the green hills of Manx land stand sharply against the clear blue sky, glorious sunshine has brought thousands of people to the grandstand." Fleetwood was one of the ports where enthusiasts could board the boat for the island, and was a popular embarkation point from the once-famous fishing port for riders and spectators, especially those from north and east Lancashire. Without wishing to appear to be writing a travel brochure for the Isle of Man Tourist Board, I must add that the view from the grandstand area on a warm evening takes some beating. You can look down on Douglas town, and the vision of the steamer picking its way into the harbour on a sunny evening in calm conditions is one to behold. Then it's back to reality as the first machines crackle and splutter into life for the start of the practice laps.

The heat had brought its problems for the riders, with reports of melting tar at Glen Vine, Laurel Bank, and half a mile from Sulby. This caused problems for the riders, who had to clean tar spray off their goggles and screens, as well as having to contend with swarms of flies.

Surtees was one of the first away pushing his machine into life within a couple of strides, so too Mike Hailwood on his Norton. The first mention we get of Hocking comes as he is one of 36 riders on Junior machines who will throughout the evening complete 81 laps and cover over 3000 miles between them. He was reported by the correspondent at the Highlander, just after Crosby, to be fast, but cautious on the bends. The reporter stationed at Creg-Ny-Baa suggested that many of the riders were treating the practice as "a path-finding trip."

The mention at the Highlander is the only report on Hocking's progress on the opening practice, but on the Monday morning, again in sparkling weather, the riders were out again, and so were the crowds. Hocking was one of the early starters, and got a mention in the report. "Dicky Dale on the Formula 1 BMW was an early starter, and Rhodesian Gary Hocking, hero of the French Grand Prix followed shortly afterwards on his Junior Dearden-tuned Norton." He was one of the 34 riders who completed three practice laps, his best time being 26 minutes 44.4 seconds, to put him eighth in the list of practice times, but a full two minutes behind the fastest man – none other than Manx resident Geoff Duke. Seven of the eight fastest riders were all on Nortons including, another up-and-coming youngster, Derek Minter.

At Governor's Bridge, the reporter noted that Gary was in a group of riders coming through at the same time: "Gary Hocking (Norton) seemed a little unsure of his line, probably worried about the presence of John Hartle (MV) who joined them through the hollow." The report continues "... it was Gary Hocking, coming through on his second lap who caused the biggest excitement. He overshot the braking point and headed straight for the flag marshal, who stood his ground as Gary pulled up and swung round, muttering to himself!" Despite the time spent learning the course, obviously riding at greater speed, and with other riders around him, Hocking was still discovering how to ride the TT course.

Having had a night to mull over his mistakes, Sox was out again for the Tuesday morning session, and his times, despite a report from Union Mills noting that he was only "touring," were starting to show that he was getting to grips with the course. At Governor's Bridge this time, Hocking was in the slip stream of Geoff Duke, and the reporter noted that Hocking "followed his line exactly" – no doubt determined not to make the same mistake as the previous day, he followed the expert. Hocking's best time had improved by over a minute to 25 minutes 29.8 seconds, at an average speed of 88.79mph. He was still about a minute and a half slower than John Surtees, who had now joined the Juniors in practice, but was fourth fastest on the Tuesday when *The TT Special* was pleased to note that "The Junior leader board showed a welcome feature – three Commonwealth riders in the first six. The fastest of the trio was Peter Pawson (New Zealand), with young Gary Hocking (Southern Rhodesia) just two seconds behind him on a Dearden Norton. The third Commonwealth rider was Norton-mounted Bob Brown, some seven seconds behind Hocking."

Gary was due also to ride in the Senior race on another of Reg Dearden's Nortons. He had his first practice on the bigger machine on the Wednesday afternoon session, and produced a lap averaging 113.95mph – exactly the same speed as Jim Redman. It was 18mph slower than John Hartle who was fastest on the practice session, with Surtees second.

On the Thursday evening practice Gary was back on the smaller machine, but there were no incidents reported involving him, and his time was a few seconds slower at 25 minutes 34 seconds, but at a faster average speed of 88.54mph, sixth in the list.

Friday saw another turn on the Senior bike taking 23 minutes 19.6 seconds to complete the lap – a minute and a quarter slower than the fastest man, Hartle, who once again pipped Surtees by ten seconds.

By Saturday morning, the final practice session, Gary was back on his Junior machine, which he would ride come race day on Monday, turning in a lap time of 25 minutes 52.2 seconds, at an average speed of 87.51mph.

He actually loaned his Senior bike to Bob McIntyre, who did a single lap on his AJS before returning to the pits and asking the chief scrutiniser for permission to go out on Hocking's Senior Norton. Permission was granted, as they wanted to see McIntyre qualify, so he did two laps, and the panic for the Scotsman was over.

Gary Hocking's first taste of Isle of Man TT racing came on Monday, June 1st 1959. Unfortunately there are no records of his individual laps, or mention of him in the race reports in *The TT Special*, other than his final position of 12th having taken 2 hours 55 minutes 35.2 seconds – his fastest time of the week, at his fastest average time of 90.25mph. That position would have earned him the prize of £35. Right at the end of its June 1st report on the Junior race, *The Isle of Man Times* did mention that two teams were left in the running for the team prize. Three riders were needed to form a team to represent a club, and the Matabeleland Motorcycle Club was represented by Jim Redman, Bob Anderson and Gary Hocking. The other team in the running was the Southern Isle of Man team, represented by Geoff Duke, Dave Chadwick, and George Costain. The Southern team just scraped home to win the small prize money and the trophy that went with it.

Before the race, Costain recalls he did see Hocking: "It was just friendly chit chat with me that we had in the garage, I was only an also ran in the TT." Having come 23rd to Hocking's 12th, George Costain didn't see much of Sox in the race, but recalls seeing him later. "At the end of the race at the garage where we kept our bikes for the races, before the bike had gone cold it had all been cleaned down, paintbrush and petrol and everything, and dried and polished and ready to go again. He did that himself. That was the kind of guy that he was."

The entry list was dominated by Norton machines, with a few BMWs, AJSs and two MVs, but it was the Agustas of Surtees and Hartle that dictated proceedings as expected. Surtees won in a new record time of 2 hours 46 minutes 8 seconds, at an average speed of 95.38mph. It was Surtees third successive TT win. Hartle came second after Bob McIntyre's AJS gave up the ghost at the end of lap four, following a tremendous scrap with Alastair King.

Despite his practising on the Senior machine, Gary Hocking was beaten by the weather before he could ride in the Senior race. As the fans awoke on the Saturday morning for the climax of the TT, so the clouds were down and there was no possibility of racing. For the first time in 25 years, the event was rescheduled for the Monday, but as Hocking had previously committed himself to riding at Karlskoga in Sweden he had to pull out. His first Isle of Man TT was over, but he had the desire for more. Reg Dearden later told a reporter how Gary had regretted having to leave the island before he could race in the Senior TT, as he was really at home in wet weather!

Such was Gary Hocking's desire to do well at the Isle of Man TT that, after joining the MV team, he persuaded the bosses to send him over with a machine to get further practice on the Mountain Course. Bear in mind he had already spent the winter of 1958 over there, and ridden in the '59 races, but such was his determination and attention to detail in his preparation that he felt further practice was needed.

By 1960, thanks to the pressure of Hocking, Nobby Clark was becoming trusted a little more by the MV mechanics and officials, so he was despatched to the Isle of Man with a road-going version of the 196cc machine. "I rode the machine from the MV factory to the Milan central station," said Clark. "From there I caught the train right through to London, where I changed to the train for Liverpool. There I caught the ferry across to the island. The bike was for Gary to ride around the circuit to learn more about it."

With Monza being the home training and testing track for the MV organisation, Hocking and the other riders would have known this course well enough, but there is no record of Hocking taking steps to familiarise himself with any other circuit the way he did the Isle of Man. Hocking practised on the course on the bike delivered by Clark, then crossed the Channel to ride in the French Grand Prix, before returning to the island again for the 1960 TT as an MV rider, and with his contract to ride the smaller machines he would taste success for the first time.

On the Saturday practice, larger-than-ever-before crowds gathered at the many vantage points, free of charge, and watched the riders complete 278 laps, or almost 10,500 miles, in perfect conditions. Things didn't go well for Sox when the gearbox gave out on his 250. In the Monday session, though, despite the fog that restricted visibility from the Mountain to Windy Corner, he smashed the previous lap record (78.21mph) by no less than six seconds on his 125cc machine. Fans watching at Governor's Bridge took timings as the machines came into view and disappeared again between the hairpin and Glencrutchery Road, although there is no reference to the total distance measured. Whatever it was, the fastest machines covered the timed length in 11.2 seconds, with Sox only managing 12. However, the overall 84.41mph of Hocking was the fastest, giving him a lap time of 29 minutes 42.6 seconds, with Mike Hailwood on his Ducati just under eight seconds slower. But that was only practice.

When entries closed for the Lightweight and 125cc races, Hocking was named in both classes, along with 41 other riders in the 125cc and 65 in the 250cc. All five races – 125, 250, 350, 500cc and side cars – were to be held over the Mountain Course for the first time since 1925, and for the first time in the history of the TT there were 300 entries in all the races. Other notable facts were that there was only one previous winner in the 125cc race: Carlo Ubbiali. The organisers were also pleased to see so many overseas entries, with 59 of the 180 riders coming from overseas, not including Ireland. Statistics also showed that when it came to the different machines, there were nine different makes in the 125cc race, whilst in the 250, Hocking's MV was one of 24 different makes of machine. It was the first 125cc race over the Mountain Course since 1953, and the first 250cc race since 1954 over the long course. The road at Bray Hill had been resurfaced, as had other areas of the course, which was expected to result in even faster times.

There was plenty to grab the attention of the thousands of enthusiasts who made the trip across the Irish Sea on their annual pilgrimage to the TT races, which were proving as popular as ever. *The Isle of Man Examiner* reported that the whole of the Steam Packet fleet of boats would be at sea, "for the eve of TT invasion holiday makers." *The Examiner* advertised the legal notices of road closures and parking restrictions; the excitement was building as the most special week in the island's year drew ever closer.

As a result of the fast practice timings, the opening Monday of the race week was expected to be something special, with three races: 125cc over three laps starting at 10.00am, and whatever the state of the race it would be finished by 12.00pm; at 12.30pm it was the turn of the sidecars, and the 250s would be off at three on their five laps, with a 6:10pm deadline finish.

Monday dawned and Hocking was ready. The riders, who used to set off at a mass start, were now being despatched in pairs, and Sox was paired with Hailwood on his Ducatti. Geoff Davidson, writing in *The TT Special*, thought that the entry, reduced to 33 riders because of withdrawals, on nine different makes of machine, and half of them from overseas, was the biggest field ever for the 125s, and anticipated that it would be the most exciting 125cc race ever held.

Sox had written letters inside his fairing: "O-H-T-E-U-A-C." Later it emerged that this was a code for the riders he would lookout for. 'O' for himself, 'H' for Hailwood, 'T' for Taveri, 'E' for Templeman, 'U' for Ubbaili, 'A' for Anderson, and finally 'C' for Crooks. It shows the preparation that Hocking put into his races. The weather report five minutes before the start stated that "visibility is good, but there are strong winds on the Mountain Section." With four minutes to go a maroon is fired, startling no doubt if the riders were not watching what was going on, but the noise must have set the heart racing, and at ten o'clock precisely the race is on. Hocking is away the quicker with Hailwood in close attendance.

It is hard to think of another sport, other than perhaps tobogganing, where a competitor sets off and can be stopped by no-one. No-one can remind them of the dangers, if they needed reminding. No-one can plead with them to think again and return to the safety of the paddock. They are away at breakneck speed in a burst of smoke, and the scream of their machine down Bray Hill.

Like the majority of people who have never had the opportunity or the courage to ride the TT course, it is interesting to gather the experiences of others to describe what it is like to go blazing down Bray Hill at the start of a race. Bob Dowty did it many times but says that even watching can be a frightening experience. "It is a scary place. In my day we used to go down at 120, now they go down at 180 even 190, it's frightening to see them, but when you are on the bike you are so concentrating on what you are doing, finding the right line and the right points, your mind is just concentrating on the job; so you are not frightened at all." Dowty uses the analogy of the big dipper where he said he was scared out of his wits because there was nothing he could do as the machine was in charge. "Going down Bray Hill was a cinch compared to that, as my mind was just concentrating on what I was doing. If you start thinking of other things or what might happen then you are in trouble."

A taxi driver who had been a regular rider in the TT races explained that when he was waiting at the start, he would look up and down the line of riders thinking

"Maybe one or two of us might not come back today." The dangers were well known and accepted, but he agreed that concentration was vital.

According to the report of the 125cc race of 1960, in under six minutes Hocking was timed through Ballacraine about two seconds ahead of Hailwood, and was leading at Kirk Michael, with Taveri second and Ubbiali, who had started 20 seconds after Hocking, third. Reports quickly reach the grandstand that Hailwood had come off at Glen Helen and been forced to retire. Hocking lead Ubbiali by five seconds through Ramsey, with Taveri third. Hocking completed his first lap out in front of the field on the road in 26 minutes 50.8 seconds, but Ubbiali was the race leader with a first lap time of 26 minutes 38.2 seconds, four seconds behind Hocking on the road, but with a 16-second time advantage.

Ubbiali did his second lap in a new record average speed of 83.13mph and now had a lead of about 18 seconds. The third and final lap saw no change in position, as Hocking crossed the line first on the road with Ubbiali about five yards behind, but as he had started 20 seconds after Gary, Ubbiali was the comfortable winner of the £75 prize money by just under 20 seconds. With Taveri in third place it gave MV a clean sweep in the first three places, and the manufacturer's team prize.

After the race, Gary said that it had been a very easy ride with no trouble at all. Meanwhile, the MV mechanics stripped down the three machines for examination as they always did after racing, and remained very secretive when the press was allowed into the paddock. No one was allowed anywhere near Taveri's machine.

At this time documentary recordings were made of races – they may still be – and the commentary plus interviews were put together with the co-operation of Graham and Murray Walker. This was then produced as a vinyl LP record, some of which these days are highly sought-after. On the sleeve of the record, Graham Walker wrote a synopsis of the featured races, which, on part one of the 1960 series includes the 250cc race that was Hocking's next appointment.

He mentioned that Tarquino Provini, winner of the 1958 and '59 races over the shorter Clypse course, hoped to become the first man to win three Lightweight TTs in a row. Walker noted, though, that there were two other riders – Carlo Ubbiali and Gary Hocking – who might just be as determined to win as the Italian. Both were on MVs, but were free to ride their own races independent of any factory instructions. So the scene was set for the final race of what had been so far an enthralling and exciting opening day.

The five-lap, 187-mile race was deemed the most open of the three first day events, and with the return to the Mountain Course and an increase to five laps, it had become far more credible. In his introduction to the excellent LP record of the 1960 250cc race, Graham Walker suggested it would be one of the finest 250cc events since the TT began in 1922, for two reasons: the return to the 37.75-mile Mountain Course, and because there had never been a higher quality entry. Of the 41 starters, 18 were on works or semi-works machines from six different factories.

One of the biggest crowds ever seen on the island was spread around the course at favourite vantage points. As with the other races, the riders were being sent off in pairs, and the whole field would be racing within five and a half minutes of the first pair being flagged away. The weather was not quite as good as the morning race, although the rain that fell towards the end of the sidecar race had stopped, and the roads were dry. There were a lot of black clouds about, but the wind had dropped.

Fifteen minutes before the start time, as the riders pushed their bikes out onto the grid, the light rain began again, making the surface that much more slippery. On the stroke of three o'clock, Tarquino Provini on his Morini was away on his own, as second fastest qualifier Ernst Degner's MZ was one of the non-starters. Next came the three MVs of Ubbiali, Taveri, and Hocking, who was paired with the MZ of John Hempleman. At Union Mills, three miles from the start, the order of the first five remained the same, but Hocking was reported to be riding "like a man possessed" and he had cut well into the ten-second gap between himself and the two riders in front of him. Such was Hocking's determination to set a pace that by Ramsey, he was in front on the road and had something like a 22-second lead over Provini, with Ubbiali three seconds behind. That lead continued throughout the first lap, which Gary completed in 24 minutes 41.8 seconds at 91.70mph – a Lightweight TT record, and faster by five seconds than anything produced in practice.

Graham Walker was full of praise for Gary's performance. "Throwing caution to the winds, he risked everything through the treacherously greasy twists and turns of the notorious Glen Helen section to gain a vital first lap lead of 23 seconds over Provini, who, in turn, was only three seconds ahead of Ubbiali."

By Ramsey on lap two, the lead had increased to 55 seconds in race time, and once the leader went through Parliament Square the fans had to wait another 35 seconds before second-placed Provini appeared, such was Hocking's domination. "No other machine," said The Daily Times report, "could live with the MV." At Keppel Gate he was reported as "taking an extremely fast line through and using every inch of the road, in terrific style, with Provini lagging behind."

The second lap set another record, this time of 93.96mph, and on lap three another record (94.24mph) had the fans going mad, and the course commentators could not conceal their excitement at what was happening in front of them. With this kind of riding and the machine going like a dream, it was only natural that eventually speeds would settle down, as Hocking realised that if nothing went wrong the race was his. At the end of his penultimate lap, his lead over Provini on the road was 40 seconds – in race time an advantage of a minute – and his average lap speed had dropped to a mere 93.53mph.

Now Ubbiali decided he would go for the finish line, and on his fourth lap he set yet another new lap record at 94.35mph, increasing it to 95.51mph on his final lap. The Daily Times called it "the crowning sensation of a terrific race." Walker

Continued page 129

Still not entrusted with the big bikes, in 1960 Gary Hocking also rode in the Lightweight race, in which he came second behind team-mate Carlo Ubbiali, with Luigi Taveri third in an MV 1.2.3. (Courtesy Tony Breeze Racing Photos IOM)

In 1961 Gary Hocking suffered the cold Isle of Man weather. He set a fashion trend with his trademark duffle coat.

Dicky Dale's wife, Phyllis, took pity on Gary in the cold weather of 1961, and knitted him this jumper. (Billy James Collection)

Over Ballaugh Bridge on the MV 350cc during the 1961 Junior race. (Courtesy Tony Breeze Racing Photos IOM)

The end of the 350cc race at the 1961 TT. Hocking was second to Phil Read on his Norton. Hocking's MV is covered in oil, and it was an achievement to get the machine home. Apparently, the boy in the cap is a young Barry Sheene. (Courtesy Duncan Hocking)

Always happy to sign autographs, by 1961, Gary Hocking relaxes in some rare sunshine on a bale of straw. (Courtesy Duncan Hocking)

Mike Hailwood (3) leads Gary Hocking (6) at Governor's Bridge, in the 1962 Junior TT.

Lining up to begin practice for the 1962 Senior TT. Behind Gary Hocking is Ron Langston.

The wreckage of Gary Hocking's MV 4 after his collision with Graham Smith, after which his machine burst into flames. Thankfully, Andrea Magni worked hard on the main machine to get it ready for the Senior race. (Courtesy forums.autosport.com)

Gary Hocking with Mike Hailwood. Their relationship was not always this cordial.

Relieved to see her son safely home
after he had won the 1962 500cc
race, Gary had promised his mother
and father that he would retire after
this race.
(Courtesy Duncan Hocking)

A smile of satisfaction and a job
done. Holding the Senior trophy in
1962.

The telegram from Count Agusta sent after Gary Hocking won the 1962 Senior TT. (Courtesy Duncan Hocking)

Gary Hocking on the Norton he rode during the summer series in South Africa in 1959-60. Here, he chases Jim Redman, also on a Norton, during the 500cc race at East London on New Year's Day. Hocking's Norton had a three inch crack in the crankcase, which is probably why Redman had wins in both the 350cc and 500cc races that day.
(Picture Alton Berns; courtesy Robert Young)

Battered and aged this Norton might have been, with a crack in the cam, but, according to Gary Hocking, it went like a rocket.

For the summer series of 1960-61, MV did allow the MV 4 to go to South Africa. Here, at the start of the 500cc race at Roy Hesketh, Gary Hocking (1) leads away, with Peter Pawson (4, New Zealand), Paddy Driver (3), Jim Redman (2), and Dickie Dale (5). (Courtesy Robert Young.)

Gary Hocking takes the 500cc MV Agusta 4 through Angels Angle in the 1961 Durban Centenary Handicap at the Roy Hesketh. At the previous meeting at the circuit he had won the National Handicap, to clinch the 1960 South African 500cc championship. (Courtesy Robert Young)

The fans were thrilled to see their local hero when he returned in 1960-61 with the MV 4, which became the big attraction.
(Courtesy Agusta Museum, Samarate, Italy)

A perfect line out of the bend at the Belvedere circuit in Salisbury. (Billy James Collection)

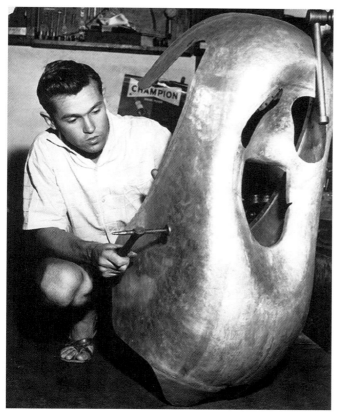

Having moved into the Chorley family home, this didn't mean that Valerie saw much more of her boyfriend. He beat out a sheet of aluminium into the shape of the fairing for the AJS 7R. (Billy James Collection)

Alan Harris took this photograph of the finished fairing on the AJS 7R at Kumalo. (Picture Alan Harris; courtesy Billy James)

The sun glints off the front wheel of the AJS 7R at Kumalo. (Billy James Collection)

The fairing obviously worked, as Gary Hocking is congratulated on winning the Lions International Race at Kumalo on November 6th, 1961, beating Jim Redman into second place and Paddy Driver into third. (Billy James Collection)

Gary Hocking leading the way again on the AJS 7R at Westmead. Note how close the crowd is to the track, and that the safety barrier consists of a piece of rope!

The AJS 7R without the fairing. (Courtesy Morag Tritt)

The Ridgeback: the combination of a Triumph 650 engine in a Manx Norton frame. (Courtesy Morag Tritt)

Gary with girlfriend Valerie Chorley, being welcomed by the Mayor of Bulawayo, Jack Payne, when he returned in 1961 as world champion. (Billy James Collection)

Hocking enjoys a soft drink with John Wells, on his return to Rhodesia as world champion. Wells, to Gary's left, helped Hocking throughout his career, and gave him contacts in Europe.

When he returned as world champion, Gary was invited to mix with the important people of Rhodesia. Here he is photographed in a white suit; the Governor of Rhodesia, Sir Humphrey Gibbs OBE, is stood behind in the dark suit, fourth from the right, with Lt Col H B Everard, Chairman of the Rhodesia Motor Sports Association, stood centre. (Billy James Collection)

Gary Hocking in the Tim Parnell Lotus 21 Climax at Oulton Park,
1962 – his first meeting in Europe in a car. (Courtesy Robert Young)

Gary Hocking chasing Jack
Brabham through the old
Esso bend at Oulton Park.
Brabham was driving the
more powerful Lotus-Climax
V8. Hocking would be forced
to retire with engine trouble
on lap 62.
(Billy James Collection)

Gary Hocking with a scrutineer before practice for the South African Grand Prix. The official has his hand on what would later kill Gary Hocking by smashing through his helmet.

A local spectator at the Westmead circuit examines the wreckage of Gary Hocking's car in disbelief. (Courtesy *Bulawayo Chronicle*)

TRIBUTES TO GARY HOCKING

This is what was left (above) of the Lotus Climax V8 racing car in which the Rhodesian motor ace, Gary Hocking (25), crashed and was fatally injured during a practice session at the Westmead circuit, Mariannhill, yesterday. Travelling at about 100 m.p.h., the car left the track, somersaulted over a tree and smashed into a tree stump. The lower picture, showing Gary Hocking in pensive mood during practice at Westmead, was one of the last taken of the young racer.

THE news of the tragic death at Westmead yesterday afternoon of Gary Hocking, Rhodesia's top sportsman, during a practice run for today's second Natal Grand Prix, was front-paged by the London and provincial evening newspapers and given prominence in every radio and television news bulletin.

Gary's parents, Mr. and Mrs. Arthur Hocking, who live in Newport, Monmouthshire, heard the news on the radio before friends had time to break it to them.

The Federal High Commissioner in London, Sir Alfred Robinson, who was in Brussels, sent them a cable of condolences ending "All Rhodesians will mourn with you."

Reg Dearden, doyen of former T.T. riders, said: "Gary was the most popular sportsman the Commonwealth has ever sent to Britain. He was a brilliant boy who certainly would have got to the top in Grand Prix racing."

* * *

At the Steering Wheel Club in London's West End, international rendezvous of racing drivers, where Hocking had been welcomed by the top-class drivers as a competent, modest and most likeable newcomer, one member said: "This is the worst thing

Bulawayo Chronicle article of 22nd December, 1962, reporting Gary Hocking's death.

Gary Hocking's gravestone in Christchurch cemetery, Newport, South Wales. His father was also buried here, but his mother died in America.
(Author's collection)

Some of those who attended the 50-year memorial of Gary Hocking's death in 2012. Ken Robas is fourth from the right in the front row. Sitting on the bike is Billy James, who provided many photographs for this book, and behind him in the black cap is Nobby Clark. Dave Harris, who organised the event, is standing fourth from the left in the back row.
(Courtesy Morag Tritt)

continued with his description: "Having thus rattled the opposition, and riding on the hairline which separates safety from catastrophe, Hocking held onto his initial advantage, whilst behind him raged a titanic battle in which Ubbiali, with a record last lap took second place from Provini in the closing minutes of the race."

As news was reported that Hocking was at Signpost Corner almost within sight of the finish, the crowd in the grandstand was on its feet, and there was a huge cheer as he took the chequered flag, finishing the race in 2 hours 53 seconds at 93.64mph – a record average speed. Carlo Ubbiali was second 1 minute 33.4 seconds behind, and, deprived of his hat-trick, Provini came home third, 1 minute 44.6 seconds behind the winner.

The headlines in *The TT Special* read "Hocking's Record 250 TT," under which it was added that Ubbiali had set a new lap record of 95.51mph. *The Isle of Man Daily Times* headline read "Hocking wins a 'Sizzling' 250 – Bang go the records."

Hocking was delighted with his victory, but was sorry that he hadn't been informed about Ubbiali's record lap. He had been told to slow down some way before the end of the race. That might have been a wise instruction, as when the machines were stripped down in the examination enclosure it was discovered that a valve spring was missing. Gary thought it may have broken coming out of Governor's Bridge as he made the dash for the line.

The Mayor of Douglas, TD Lewis, presented the trophies in the Villa Marina gardens, in front of the biggest crowd ever to attend a first day prize-giving ceremony. Gary said how he could not put into words how proud he was to have won such a great race. Typically for him, he also thanked the organisers and helpers.

As a result of the wins for MV, the advertisers were quickly into action to impress upon the motorcycling public the part their products had played in the successes. Wellworthy Piston Rings announced how all the winners had been powered by its products. The machines had been fuelled and oiled by Mobil, boasted the full-page advert. Lodge plugs were responsible for sparking John Surtees' engines into life, and both the 125cc and 350cc races had been won on Avon tyres.

Hocking also turned in a very competitive practice time for the Junior race, but it was something of a surprise, and a disappointment following his performance on Monday, that he was amongst the list of non-starters. No official reason was given, but there was speculation that he either blew up the only serviceable machine available to him, or once again it concerned the politics of MV. There was a rumour that Sox had upset the Gallarate management by winning the 250cc race on Monday, his victory having prevented Ubbiali an Italian double on the lightweights; small-minded, but, as *The TT Special* reminded its readers, "he who pays the piper calls the tune."

The TT Special produced by *The Isle of Man Examiner* was a fantastic publication for the fans who made the trip to the island. They were unique to the TT races, but were superb examples of local newspaper journalism. They are still produced for the modern day TT, but not as frequently as back in Gary Hocking's day. Then they were full of practice reports, with a full list of practice times, lists of entries, details of every rider taking part, articles about machines, historical races, off the course articles; everything from the weather to the road conditions kept the enthusiast informed. These can now be downloaded from the Manx Museum website, and are well worth a look.

In the 12th June edition in 1961, Gary was featured as one of the stars of the previous season's races. The article doesn't tell us anything new about Sox, as it regurgitates his past history in races, but it does mention again his non-start in the 1960 350cc race, for which he was entered. Once again, though, the theory was put forward that his withdrawal had something to do with small-minded people upset because he denied Carlo Ubbiali a Lightweight Italian double.

So, now Hocking was a TT star with a win under his belt, he could look forward to the 1961 series of races for which he was entered in all four solo classes, and by now he was on the Privat MVs.

The first practice session of 1961 was on the Friday before racing began, and was dominated by two events: first, the domination of the Lightweight class by the Japanese Hondas, especially Luigi Taveri's lap which was close to Ubbiali's lap record of the previous year, and second, Hocking's near 100mph lap on the Senior MV. The Auto Cycle Union decided for the first time not to record any rider's first lap times, even if they had ridden around the course before on a different machine. This was to encourage riders to take it easy on their first lap, and get to know the course before they tried to produce competitive times. Needless to say, 'go easy' wasn't on the mind of one Gary Stuart Hocking, who had never ridden in a Senior TT before, but soon dispelled any suspicions that he might not be able to handle the big MV around the Mountain Course. He did a time of 22 minutes 42 seconds at 99.73mph for his best lap – just under a minute quicker than anyone else. Hocking was reported as "very fast" through Braddan Bridge.

Gary was out again for the Saturday morning session, where he turned in a time of 23 minutes for his best lap of the three completed. Reports from observers at Governor's Bridge said he went through "very smoothly and quickly." All reports of Hocking's practice laps were complimentary, with phrases like "beautifully handled, very fast," and "fast and furious." On the Wednesday session, Hocking achieved average laps of 99.74mph on his 500cc machine and 95.66mph on the Junior – the fastest by a Junior machine to date. He was now getting a reputation as a fashion trendsetter as well, often seen waiting around in the cold conditions wearing his hooded duffle coat.

By the Thursday session things were really hotting up, and one headline announced that Hocking had recorded the first 100mph practice lap of the 1961 meeting, and his first ton on the 500. He had begun the session on his 350, but at Kirk Michael his engine had seized, and after a car journey back to the paddock he was away again on the 500, turning in a lap speed of 101.06mph There was a warning in the report from Sulby Bridge that Hocking had gone rather too close to the wall for comfort, but he was "stylish" and heralded by a "glorious, frightful noise." With his times in practice, Gary was being tipped in some quarters for a Junior/Senior double.

Once again, huge crowds flocked to the island, with over 400 enthusiasts arriving in Douglas for the opening Monday. Such was the interest that the BBC was to provide its biggest ever coverage, with a crew of 25 and no fewer that 14 camera positions. Filmed reports would be shown on *Sportsview*, the mid-week sports programme, and in the news on Monday, Wednesday, and Friday. Murray Walker and George Carr would provide commentary for the BBC North 25-minute review of the week's racing, and there would be 17 radio reports on the Home Service, the Light Programme and Network Three.

First race on the Monday was the Lightweight 125cc, but there was no Gary Hocking in the line-up even though he was in the programme. No explanation can be found as to why he didn't start – he hadn't posted a practice time either. Nobby Clark, who was on the island by this time, thinks that Gary had always felt he was too heavy to ride the 125cc machines, and may well have decided simply not to race in this class. As the entries had to be in well before the races, it would be safer for a rider to enter and then withdraw, than not to enter and regret it.

There was obviously nothing wrong with Hocking, as in the 250cc class on the Monday afternoon he was the only MV rider to do battle with the Hondas. He set off paired with Mike Hailwood chasing Bob McIntyre, and by the time the riders reached Sulby, Hailwood had a 100-yard lead over Hocking, but by the end of the first lap the positions were reversed as the riders screamed past the grandstand. They were still behind McIntyre who had set a new lap record and was about 2mph faster than Hocking.

So close was the race that by Sulby on the second lap just 30 seconds separated the first five riders. Problems struck the MV though at Kirk Michael on lap three, and although Gary continued for another couple of miles at a cruising speed until he reached Ballaugh, his race had ended.

By the Wednesday Gary could probably have dispensed with the duffle coat as temperatures were promised to be between 65 and 70 degrees and conditions just about perfect for the Junior race. He had set the fastest time in practice, at 95.66mph, but it was suggested that the Junior practice speeds had been 'disappointing' for some reason. Now in the race it was thought that Hocking and perhaps one or two others would break the ton. *The TT Special* in its usual informative way had given a bit of a history of the Junior race, which was the first motorcycle race to ever be held over the Mountain Course back in 1911, and was won at an average speed of 41.45mph; Gary had done double that and more in practice.

Hocking got away to his traditional quick start and by Ramsey he had already built up a substantial lead over Mike Hailwood and Derek Minter, which had increased to 42 seconds by Signpost Corner. He roared past the grandstand flat on the tank with the sun glinting off his silver helmet, the flame red MV purring and yet also snarling. He completed his first lap from a standing start eight seconds over the 23 minutes, at an average speed of 97.80mph – if he got pushed at any point, those who thought the ton might be on would be proved right.

The second lap was even quicker: 22 minutes 41 seconds, a new Junior record. The gap over Hailwood had increased and was now over a minute. The commentator at Keppel Gate got very excited – as Hocking took the curves he lifted his hand from the bar and turned to look down at his engine, which sounded as though it had cut out on one cylinder. The spectators at the grandstand listened for the sound of the MV as it went down through the gears and then accelerated away from the dip at Governor's Bridge, and at the end of the third lap Hocking pulled into the pits for a fuel stop and also to change a plug.

This stop cost him a minute, in which time Hailwood had also arrived for his refuelling – a stop which only lasted 24 seconds, so Hailwood was now trailing by only half a minute. By Sulby Bridge, just over half way round the fourth lap, Hailwood was reported to be in the lead on the road, and Hocking had another nervous glance down at his rear tyre at Keppel Gate. What he saw wasn't encouraging. He had dropped an exhaust valve and oil was spraying over the back wheel.

With four laps completed Hocking was in real trouble. By Signpost Corner he had not only lost the lead on the road, but was now almost a minute behind Hailwood on the clock. Firing on three cylinders, the classic sound of the MV had now given way to a splutter and a misfire, and Hocking was now coming under pressure from Phil Read. Despite his problems, though, Sox still turned in a fourth lap at 95.19mph

By the end of lap four Hailwood's lead was two minutes, and Read was 20 seconds ahead of Hocking on the clock. As they came through the grandstand, Hailwood raised his hand as if to signal to the mechanics that all is well, whilst 62 seconds later Hocking comes through with a simple nod to his pit.

Having won the 125cc and 250cc races earlier in the week, Hailwood looked set to make history by becoming the first rider to win three TTs in a week, but fate played its hand late in the race. At Ramsey on the final lap it was Hocking who came through first, but with Read close behind, the Englishman was leading the race. There was no sign of Hailwood who at Milntown, just 14 miles from the finish line, suffered a broken gudgeon pin and was out of the race. Hailwood would have to wait for his piece of history.

As the MV struggled out of Ramsey and started the climb up to the Mountain, Read overtook Hocking and by the top of the Mountain had a 40-second lead on the road. He could coast to a standing ovation from the grandstand at the finish to win on his first appearance in a Junior TT. Hocking did manage to hold off Minter and Ralph Renson to take second place, but his machine by now was covered in oil from a broken cam-box, and he reported that his problems had started halfway around his second lap. With that in mind, to bring the bike home at an average speed of 94.25mph showed his skill, and ability to nurse the machine to the finish.

No fewer than five boat-loads of enthusiasts, estimated to be about eight or nine thousand, arrived in Douglas Harbour on the Friday morning to watch the Blue Riband of motorcycle racing – the 500cc Senior TT. The races remain vital to the Isle of Man economy, but these days, the way the enthusiasts travel and where they stay has changed considerably. Back in the early 1960s, there were far fewer motorbikes brought over by the fans, as all bikes had to be craned onto and off the ships. It wasn't until the Manx Maid came into service in 1962 that cars and vans could be rolled on and off. As a result, few riders or factory teams brought their vans onto the island – they brought only what they needed. But they still came in their thousands on foot. Once they had landed at Douglas a fleet of coaches was waiting, which took many of them on a tour around the course, whilst others were dropped off at vantage points around the 37.75 miles. Some would spend a few pounds in the pubs, but many would watch the races, climb back onto the coaches, and be taken back to the harbour to catch the returning day trip. They would have spent little or no money on the island.

Motorcycle magazines would often arrange day trips, taking the fans by train to Liverpool then by boat to Douglas. Fans came from other areas and other countries as well. The Isle of Man Examiner reported that "the fleet would be at sea for the eve-of-TT invasion. The Lady [of Mann] would be on the Liverpool run during the weekend as would the Ben [My-Chree], between them making twelve cross-channel journeys." The Manxman would bring a charter from Dublin, and the Mona's Isle would bring a charter from Belfast.

Also, years ago fans not on day trips would take rooms in the local hotels and B&Bs. Many of these have closed down since the tourist trade on the island has diminished. Now, many fans will camp, but, wherever they stay, these are the people who put money into the island.

However they travelled, a walk along Douglas promenade to look at the bikes, many of which would be taking part in the races, was an essential part of any trip to the Isle of Man. Also, several owners' clubs would hold meetings during the TT period, and, of course, there was the usual holiday entertainment at the many ballrooms or theatres that attracted the attention of visitors.

So, the scene was set for the major event of the week. It was thought that without the MV works entry, the competition would be much more open and interesting. On his private entry, Gary Hocking was the only MV representative up against 62 Nortons, 24 AJS Matchless, and four BSAs, a dozen of which could be classed as possible winners. In 1960, John Surtees, on his MV, had smashed the opposition, winning at 102.44mph and setting the record lap at 104.08mph. With only one MV racing in 1961, no wonder the pundits thought it would be more open. Hocking had set the fastest lap in practice at 22 minutes 24 seconds, 101.06mph, but that was 39 seconds slower than Surtees' winning time the previous year. Experts put Surtees' extra speed down to his individual cornering style, in which he used a technique of hanging inside his machine, which kept it slightly more upright. This enabled him to use more throttle, and was a style no one had ever seen Hocking adopt.

Hailwood was 26 seconds slower, and Minter another 21 seconds behind Hailwood. But any of those three were possible winners; you could also have added Tom Phillis on his Norton Twin, or fellow Norton rider Phil Read.

The weather wasn't perfect, and the travelling marshal reported that after heavy overnight rain there were some wet patches on the course at the Nook and Governor's Bridge. Hocking set off in partnership with Bob McIntyre, but by the Sulby Bridge the first man into view was Hocking, crouched low behind the screen of his Gallarate screamer, ten yards ahead of McIntyre. Hailwood followed the Scot, but by Ramsey with Hocking still leading, Hailwood had overtaken McIntyre. Hocking still led at the Bungalow, the 31-mile mark, and after the Signpost Corner those on the grandstand listened for the sound of the MV dropping through the gears for the dip at Governor's Bridge.

Coming through the grandstand at the end of the first lap, the lead over Hailwood was five seconds on the road, but three times that on the clock. Despite his lead, Gary was nearly half a minute outside John Surtees' 1960 time, but both the first two riders averaged over the ton for their first lap from a standing start. Hocking's MV was now being chased by no fewer than five Nortons, but just 44 seconds covered the first half a dozen riders.

At Sulby there was the first sign of problems for Hocking, with the commentator reporting his machine as smoking when he accelerated away, but still a hundred yards ahead of Hailwood. The order continued as the riders swerved around Ramsey, up the climb to the Mountain and on past Windy Corner, through Keppel Gate and downhill to Creg-ny-Baa.

Coming through the grandstand there was no sign of smoke now, as Hocking set off down Bray Hill on lap three, where the running order continued. However, at the end of that lap both Hocking and Hailwood pulled into the pits to refuel, and, as Hailwood's pit was further down the road than the MV setup, Hailwood briefly 'led' the race.

As in previous events, Hocking's pit stop was slower than his rival's, and he lost almost all his 29-second advantage. Back on the circuit, Hocking pounded his way through Sulby, and, through the right and left at Ramsey's Parliament Square, and at the Mountain Box on lap four, Hocking had restored his lead to 15 seconds – 25 seconds on the clock, as he started ten seconds behind Hailwood. At Keppel, Hocking took the bend wider than normal in the gusty wind, and just as he did on Wednesday in the Junior race he looked down at the rear tyre.

At the end of lap four there was a shock for the huge crowd gathered at the grandstand: Hocking came into the pit for a second time, a stop that cost 44 seconds and handed Hailwood the lead, not helped by Sox missing a gear as he set off again.

Hocking and Hailwood arrived at Parliament Square, Ramsey. The fans braving the conditions and the climb to the Mountain Box welcomed Hailwood, but there was no sign of Gary Hocking – clearly something had gone wrong with the bike. He appeared almost two and a half minutes after Hailwood, limping up the mountain, and had already given up second place to his friend and rival, Tom Phillis. One of the problems was put down to the throttle sticking open, but, according to the report in *Motorcycle News,* "a load of mechanical problems had cramped his style almost from the start." At the end of lap five, fourth on the road, Hocking pulled into the pits for another disappointing end to a 1961 race.

History shows that Hailwood did write his name into the record books by winning, thus becoming the first rider to win three TT races in a week. At least the record books also show that, for this race, Hocking recorded the fastest lap – 22 minutes 3.6 seconds, at 102.62mph. But for him it was a disappointing end to his 1961 TT. One second place, one non-starter, and two failures to finish. The 'failures' of that year's TT thankfully didn't disrupt his achievement of becoming world champion at 350 and 500cc at the end of the 1961 season.

9

The beginning of the final lap

I T MAY SEEM strange to title this chapter in such a negative way, when in what would be his final appearance in the TT races Gary achieved his ultimate goal, a Senior win. But events both on and off the track would see the end of his relationship with motorbikes.

In 1962 Gary Hocking returned to the Isle of Man as an even bigger attraction, a double world champion. This time there would be no dabbling in all four classes. Hocking was going for the big two: the 350cc and the 500cc classes only. His licence number was 2813.

He started his first practice session on the senior bike in a way *The TT Special* described as "effortless, so skilfully did he handle the powerful MV." He lapped at over the 'ton' at 101.94 in 22 minutes 12.4 seconds. The Saturday practice went well, but on the Monday disaster struck. Sox was travelling at about 140mph when he came around the left-hand bend at Ballacrye, 18 miles into the lap. Just in front of him, but unseen by Hocking, was fellow Rhodesian Graham Smith, who was doing far less speed. The two collided, with Hocking's machine smashing into the back of Smith's Norton. Following the accident, Hocking told Nobby Clark: "He was right in my line, I had nowhere to go." Both riders fell heavily, and the MV burst into flames and was a write-off. They were taken to hospital in Ramsey, where it was discovered that Hocking was less seriously hurt than Smith, but both were kept in.

Nobby was despatched to Ramsey to see what the damage was to his friend, and was greeted by the nurses, who said to Clark: "Thank God you have come for him" – he had apparently been giving the staff absolute hell and wanted to get out. He got his way and returned to Douglas.

Gary had been lucky – not only could both riders have been killed, but he had been riding his spare MV for the practice session when he collided with Smith. When Sox and Nobby returned to Douglas, Andrea Magni was working hard preparing the racing machine for the 500. Sensibly, Hocking decided to give the Tuesday morning practice session a miss, whilst Hailwood went round on his 500cc MV at 94.27mph. Not resting for long though, Sox was back out on his 350cc for the Wednesday morning practice. He walked with a bit of a limp, but a masseur and an osteopath had given him "a real going over and he was almost one hundred per cent." According to the newspaper reports, his times suggested he was taking it easy. His first lap was over 31 minutes, his second over 36, but he explained that he was quite happy about the morning.

By Thursday afternoon, things appeared to be back to normal. The still limping Hocking set a new unofficial lap record on the 500cc MV with a "scorching" third lap of 21 minutes 43.8 seconds, at a speed of 104.18mph. This came after the mechanics had done a plug change, swapped the exhausts with another machine's, and adjusted the rear suspension.

Hocking and Hailwood were both reported as going over the mountain at 95.25mph. According to Bob Dowty, this is one of the areas of the TT course where riders can relax a little. "Coming out of Ramsey you have the Mountain mile and that is quite a long straight. You probably have a few seconds when you can relax, but if you are not careful your mind can wander. The danger then is if you don't get your concentration back in time."

There certainly appeared to be no such lack of concentration on the part of Gary Hocking, nor for that matter Mike Hailwood, as he turned in the fastest lap of the final practice session on the Friday at 22 minutes 0.2 seconds at 102.34mph – over 2mph and 28 seconds faster than Hocking – but the two MVs were 35 seconds faster than Bob McIntyre's Honda.

So, despite the crash on the Monday, practice had gone well for Sox, and he was ready for the first of his two races, the Junior TT. Here he would come up against 'team-mate' but arch rival Mike Hailwood, but, as The TT Special reported, the entry list contained "a galaxy of talent."

Before the race, Graham Walker asked both Hocking and Hailwood about their chances. Hailwood thought he was in with a good chance, but it would be a better race because there was more opposition. He also emphasised that no instructions had been given by the MV organisation about how the race should be run.

That was a point emphasised by Hocking when he spoke to Walker. "There are no instructions and I think it will be an open race this year. I am due for a break," Hocking said, remembering his rotten luck the previous year. He continued, "this week in practice we've seen that nobody has shown their paces in the 350 class. Mike and myself haven't done any fast laps at all, and Bob Mac, Redman and Phillis haven't shown their paces either. Mike and I have only done two laps on each bike and I feel we can do over the hundred straight off, but then I feel that Bob McIntyre can do likewise."

Gary spoke with a definite South African accent, but not as heavy as some from that area. It was a soft voice, with some words a slight lisp, but he comes across on this rare audio interview as a soft, gentle person with time for the interviewer.

Stan Hailwood, Mike's racing manager as well as his father, believed that his son and Gary were pretty equal riders. "The trouble," he thought, "is they might get scrapping each other," which of course is exactly what happened.

Hocking was in the third pair to set off alongside Derek Minter on a Norton, 20 seconds behind Tom Phillis and 'Franta' Stastny, but by the time Hocking reached Ballacraine, seven miles out, he had already lost ten seconds. Seven of those seconds had been recovered by the time he reached Ramsey, 24 miles into the race. By the 28-mile mark at the Mountain Box, Gary was leading the race on the road, 20 seconds ahead of Hailwood, with Tom Phillis close behind. At Signpost Corner, about a mile from the start and finish line, all three riders were together and just two seconds separated them as they crossed the line to complete the first lap, with Gary leading. Picking up the 20-second deficit he had on Phillis at the start meant that Hocking covered the first lap in 22 minutes 26.2 seconds at 100.92mph from a push-start – the first Junior 'ton,' breaking his own lap record set the previous year.

But he was dragging Hailwood along with him, and even though Hocking broke the lap record again on his second lap, setting 101.19mph, Hailwood at 100.81mph was only ten seconds behind. The ten-second gap remained at the end of the third lap, when both riders stopped at the pits to refuel. As they returned to the race they were both cheered by the crowds in the grandstand, and alongside the road leading to Bray Hill. Back to the track again, and the speeds dropped to below the 100mph mark, and at Governor's Bridge on lap four Hailwood was in the lead on the road, but with Hocking still leading the race by ten seconds. If he could hold onto his position he would win, but the pace was electrifying as the riders chased each other wheel to wheel.

By the start of lap four the only problem Hailwood and Hocking had ahead of them were the slower riders they were lapping; they were well ahead of the rest of the field. Hailwood increased the lead to something like 200 yards, but with a 20-second deficit at the start, Hocking still had the race lead of ten seconds by the end of lap four. Then the real nail-biting conclusion to the race began. Afterwards it was revealed that at about this point, Hocking began to experience engine problems and his speed started to drop. On the climb out of Ramsey up to the Mountain, the timekeepers had Hailwood seven seconds ahead of Hocking on the road, so just three seconds behind on timing. By Keppel Gate, with just over four miles to go, the gap was back up to five seconds as Hocking's engine began to recover, but then it was Hailwood's turn to encounter problems.

At Hillberry, with a mile and a bit left, Hailwood was 350 yards ahead and increasing the distance, which by the final pass of Governor's Bridge became ten seconds, as Hocking's engine dropped to two cylinders. This was unbeknown at the grandstand, where they were anticipating a dramatic finish. The fans were on their feet turning their necks to their right to catch the first glimpse of the two MVs. It was Hailwood who came into view first with a lead of something like 15 seconds, which meant that he won the Junior TT by 5.6 seconds. So far ahead were they that the fans had to wait another seven minutes before third-placed Stastny appeared!

Speaking after the race, Gary said: "On the last lap Mike started to get going to see if he could put the ten seconds between us, and I found my motor was going rather poorly. We pressed on from there, and at Ramsey I think he was leading me by about seven seconds on the road, giving me a three-second lead. Then his bike went onto three cylinders so we pressed on from there, and I noticed up the Mountain I was catching him, and I dwindled the lead down to four seconds on the road. That was giving me a six-second lead when we got down to Brandish. That is where mine went onto two cylinders, so Mike managed to use his three cylinders to gain a few seconds advantage over the line.

When he returned to the paddock and removed his crash helmet, Gary received the devastating news that his very good friend Tom Phillis had been killed in the race. On the second lap he had crashed at Laurel Bank, which Bob Dowty suggested is a particularly tricky part of the course. "The section between Ballacraine and Glen Helen, through Laurel Bank, there are a lot of different bends and gradients and cambers."

Jim Redman was a non-starter in the Junior, so he watched the race from the Grandstand and listened to the commentary. "The three of them, Hocking, Hailwood and Phillis went through together 1, 2, 3, down Bray Hill, and they were saying Hocking and Hailwood and Phillis, and then all of a sudden there was no Phillis." Redman had his wife, Marlene, with him on the island that year, and she had a nightmare the night before the race. Redman continued with the story: "She woke up saying 'I had a horrible dream last night, Tom was in a coffin and he was trying to get out and we were pushing him in, trying to close the lid.' I said 'Shit don't mention that to Tom, he doesn't need that because he will just laugh it off and ride.'"

It was a particularly difficult part of the course to gain access to, and it took the marshals some time to reach Phillis. Once they got to him they put him on a stretcher and carried him up a path to the waiting ambulance, but one of the marshals stated that when they got to the top, Phillis let out one big gasp. It was his last.

When Gary got back to the paddock and received the news about his friend, he immediately blamed himself, because Phillis had been chasing him for the lead. "I killed Tom Phillis today," he kept saying. Redman, in an attempt to console Hocking, said: "Only one person has got the throttle, and if you try too hard and crash you get killed." It may appear to be a pretty cynical way of dealing with death, but that was the way the riders had to look at the possibilities. It could be any one of them next, they knew the risks, and they accepted the risks as part of the job. Something that had been considered for sometime was the introduction of a helicopter to speed up the transfer of injured riders to hospital, and as a result of the death of Tom Phillis, some action crystallised. The following year a helicopter was introduced, sponsored by Shell and BP.

The death of his friend would have a profound effect on the life and career of Gary Hocking, and for a couple of days in June 1962, he had to contemplate his taking part in the Senior – the closing event of the TT meeting and the biggest race of the fortnight. His parents were on the island to watch the TT, and after his crash and seeing Tom Phillis killed, Gary discussed the future with his father. Arthur Hocking was certain; with not only Phillis, but so many other riders being killed, he said: "I have no doubt about the right course; give up racing." Hocking would set off in the 500cc race with one promise to his parents – he would retire.

In practice, Gary had beaten John Surtees' 1960 lap time by 1.2 seconds circulating the 37.75 miles in a time of 21 minutes 43.8 seconds at 104.18mph, 12.2 seconds faster than Mike Hailwood. Hocking was the only rider in practice to beat the 1960 record, and he and Hailwood were the only riders to beat the 'ton.'

Speaking again to Graham Walker, Hocking expressed how depressed he was about the death of Tom Phillis. "After yesterday's unfortunate business, the accident, I don't feel like racing a monster like that around here, so I am just going to wait till I get going and then see how I feel."

Asked about the differences between riding the 350cc and the 500cc machines, Hocking added: "There is a big difference, the handling for a start; there is so much power it just throws you all over the place, it is hard to hold down. You find yourself thundering along these straights and arriving too quick everywhere. It is no place to be making a mistake."

Hailwood was asked if there was any difference between the machine he was riding and that of Hocking's. "The machines are supposed to be even. As for the riders, I think he is a little better than me I am afraid to say," which was some admission.

It looked as though the race would develop into another Hocking/Hailwood battle, but the starting order this time was different, as Hocking, carrying the number 4, would start in a pair 30 seconds ahead of Hailwood, with only one pair in front of them.

We will never know the driving force behind Gary that Friday – was it revenge on Hailwood? Determination to win the Senior? The presence of the Rhodesian High Commissioner? Or was it a tribute to his close friend Tom Phillis that urged him on? Remembering what George Costain and Bob Dowty have said in previous passages, Hocking would have to put all thoughts out of his head and concentrate for the next two hours.

The 76 entries were made up of eight different makes: no fewer than 42

Nortons, 22 Matchless, four BSAs, three AJS, one Guzzi, Honda, and Triumph, and of course the two fire engines ridden by Hocking and Hailwood.

No sooner had the second pair of riders set off than Sox was beginning to pull back the ten-second deficit he had over Alan Shepherd and Ron Langston. By Ballacraine, not only had he done that, but he had also established a lead – a lead he would hold and cherish until he reached his target. Hocking had suffered so many times through bad luck, with breakdown after breakdown in the TTs, often with Hailwood being the beneficiary. This time the luck would be on Hocking's side.

Flat on the tank from the moment the MV fired up, within five miles he had open road in front of him, but Hailwood had already pulled back five of the 30-second deficit and was in hot pursuit. Seldom had a race been so exciting and contained so much passion from the very start. By Sulby, the 20-mile mark, Hailwood was two seconds up on Hocking in race time. Anticipating the challenge coming up behind him, by Keppel Gate Hocking had taken back the two seconds, and was starting, just, to pull away.

Remembering what he had said before the race about seeing how he felt, was this the point that Gary decided he was in good enough shape to go for the victory? Little did anyone know that for the first 20 miles of the race Hocking's machine had been suffering low-speed carburation, and the pilot had been forced to adjust his acceleration. He had almost stalled the engine at Quarter Bridge on the first lap. At the completion of the first 37.75 miles Hocking's time was 21 minutes 49 seconds, covered at 103.76mph. It was four seconds down on Surtees' record, but his lead was 1.6 seconds over the other MV.

Now, with riders dropping like flies with mechanical trouble, Hocking began to stretch the lead, and by the time they reached the highest point of the course for a second time, Sox had a massive 45-second advantage. As the clocks ticked around on the scoreboard showing where the riders were on the course, it seemed obvious that Surtees' two-year-old record was about to be smashed ... and as the two MVs came screaming passed the grandstand, sure enough it was. Hocking, 21 minutes 24.4 seconds, 104.55mph – no less than 20.6 seconds better than Surtees. Again he was dragging Hailwood along behind him, even beating the old record by over half a second. As other machines began to wilt under the strain of trying to keep up with the leaders, so too did the Hailwood mount. At Keppel Gate, the commentator remarked that Hailwood's riding had been "hairy," but the explanation was that Hailwood had lost bottom gear. The clutch was beginning to show signs of the strain, but when the riders came in for fuel at the end of the third lap the Englishman decided to continue. Hocking, whose refuel stop took no more than 30 seconds, reported no problems and was soon back on the road.

All eyes were now on Hailwood, whose clutch began smouldering. He eased the pace on his fourth lap hoping for the best, but his best would have been for Sox to have problems as well. No chance, as Hocking simply kept up a relentless pace. At the end of lap four Hailwood realised he was losing the battle with the clutch, and pulled into the pits. There now began one of the most remarkable pieces of pit wall engineering ever seen at a TT meeting. Andrea Magni began to dismantle the clutch as smoke poured from the old plates, and replace them with new ones – not an easy task in a garage, never mind in the pits with a race unfolding out on the track, and no doubt an impatient rider itching to get back into the fray. By now, though, Hailwood was well out of the running, and as a result of several more withdrawals as machines collapsed in the pursuit of Gary Hocking, Phil Read was up into second place with an average of 99mph.

After more than 13 minutes of frantic repairs, Hailwood's MV was put back together, and Magni rose from the bike to the rapturous applause normally reserved for a race winner. Never had there been such a reception for a mechanic in 40 years of TT racing. Hailwood was halfway down Bray Hill before the applause died down.

Behind Hocking, the carnage of machines continued. Phil Read's engine seized at Ramsey, which put Ellis Boyce into second place, but when the megaphone came off his Norton's exhaust at Ginger Hall he almost stopped, as he was worried about the strange noise the engine was making. Realising that he was in second place, the crowd urged him to continue.

He could make no impression on Hocking, though, who completed his first Senior TT win in 2 hours 11 minutes 13.4 seconds, at 103.51mph. He was ten minutes ahead of Boyce, and had turned into the pits before the reception from the crowd had even reached a crescendo, according to local reports. With a last lap of 99.54mph, Hailwood came in 12th – a position that gained him a first-class replica of the trophy lifted by Hocking. There to give her boy a hug was Sox's mother, Maj, and it was a double celebration, as Gary had been awarded the MBE in the Queen's birthday honours list. He also collected the £200 prize money.

Round three of the Hocking/Hailwood battle came at Mallory Park a week after the TT meeting. Reports in the local newspaper suggested that both riders were at their brilliant best, Hocking making the running for the first seven laps before Hailwood took the lead on lap eight, blasting past Sox and setting up a new lap record. It could be that Hocking had other things on his mind.

Nobby Clark insists that Hocking was told by Count Agusta that there wouldn't be bikes available for him in certain races in the UK. It would be company policy to promote Hailwood's rides, as he was English and the company needed to sell bikes in England!

Sox returned to Italy and kept his promise to his parents: he announced his retirement. A few weeks later, back home in Rhodesia, he sat at a desk and wrote down his thoughts. I have no hesitation here in reproducing what Gary wrote. Why not? These are the thoughts of a frustrated, lonely, individual, who was educated enough and able enough to put his thoughts into words.

Copies have been made of it, but it is quite moving to hold the original five pages, almost perfectly type-written, double-spaced, coffee-stained, and held together in one corner with a rusty staple.

By Gary Hocking

Trying to explain why a motor-cyclist suddenly makes up his mind to quit in the middle of a season when nothing particularly important has happened to speed the decision is like trying to put toothpaste back into the tube. You just cannot do it – and although I have lost count of the number of times I have been asked why I made up my mind one day in Milan to call halt to my life of speed, it is awfully difficult to put into words the hundreds of conflicting thoughts one has.

And believe me, it is even harder to put the reasons on to paper but perhaps if I can think out loud for a few hundred words, you will get some idea of why I retired.

The people who watch us out on the tracks no doubt think of most of us as determined men with a single-minded purpose – that of trying to go faster than anybody else in a continual quest for cash and glory. You see us in our leathers astride powerful machines and you forget we are just ordinary blokes who have found ourselves funnelled into a profession from which there is no escape other than quitting at the end of a long road.

The public sees us 'on duty' as it were – the Saturdays and Sundays in Europe when we race. But they never see us during the preparations for those races and probably never spare even a half-thought to the completely unnatural life expected of a works rider.

Whether you ride for the massive MV Agusta works, or Honda, or are part of a team which has its headquarters in London or Glasgow, the greatest part of one's life is spent far away from the be-flagged circuits all over Europe which spring from slumber into frenzied activity once or twice a year when a major race is staged. There is a tremendous sense of urgency about the actual races and race courses when there is a race on – but at the most, it takes up a couple of days of each week. And for the rest of the time you are alone with your thoughts.

But that is the unknown other side of a man who can be hailed as a world star when he is on duty. But when he is alone with his thoughts ...

To me, getting the contract at the end of 1959 to ride for MV was the greatest thrill in the world. But in the end, it was the hangman's noose which killed off most of my natural enjoyment of life and made my enviously sought after position one to which anyone is welcome in the future.

I am not one for the bright lights and the non-stop way of life off the track. To me, the races were there to be won, but I found it as easy to switch off the emotion and excitement after a race as it is to turn off a tap. The false world of speed, noise and smells did not stay with me for very long after the chequered flag – and then we would be off by road or plane back to the MV factory in Italy for the inquests and the continual search for more speed.

'Sox' – Gary Hocking the forgotten World Motorcycle Champion

At first, in 1960, that was great. It was part of the process of being a works rider and I love the many flattering things which went with it. Last year it was even better. The endless trips were forgotten as the huge MV organisation and I searched for the answer to make those scarlet bikes the fastest thing on two wheels and at the end of the season, Gary Hocking was a double world champion.

This year I went to Europe in April with as much enthusiasm as when I first made the journey as an unknown in 1958. But at the MV factory at Gallarate, I learned from the boss, Count Domenico Agusta, that I would only be allowed to ride in two races before the TT – one at Imola and another minor meeting nearby at Cesenatico. I arrived in Italy a week or so before Imola and got caught up in the general atmosphere which marks the start of the season, riding on practice circuits, altering this, changing that, modifying something else. I was carried along without even thinking why I was there – but after winning the 500cc event at Imola, I realised I wanted action not inactivity.

I returned home to Bulawayo, fed up with the fact I had only one race in prospect during the next five weeks. It had nothing to do with any personal plans, although a persistent rumour was around that I intended to go home to get married.

After a month in Bulawayo, I returned with the TT as my major target. A race at St Wendel in Germany – where I won the 500cc event gave me some necessary practice and the feel of the bike again and then we came to the TT races in the Isle of Man. There is an indefinable magic about the Manx circuit which offers so much of a challenge to man and machine that it is to me at least, the unquestionable home of the sport. People in Douglas and all over the island are there for one purpose in TT week – a few days of racing in which rider, mechanic, officials and spectator are experts, not just there as rubber-necking tourists. To me, the Isle of Man IS motorcycling.

Mike Hailwood beat me in the Junior TT and then I won the Senior race. Yet, within a week, I'd packed everything I had into a small bag and I was back home in Bulawayo. It is from a sun-drenched lounge here in Africa that I am writing this. Trying to explain the sudden decision which has meant several thousand pounds off my income and the end of the thrills, the glamour and the glory.

Directly, it had nothing to do with the death of Tom Phillis at the TT races. A lot of people have said his death affected me deeply and that I lost my nerve. But trying to put my thoughts in some sort of chronological order, the Phillis tragedy was not even the last straw. It certainly helped to put my thinking into focus, but I had done a great deal of thinking in the months before the TT and it is amazing how one's mind works when you have nothing but time on your hands.

I was fed up with my life in Italy. For convenience I stayed at the Hotel Popolo in Gallarate, a small town five kilometres from the MV factory. To me, a simple living youngster used to a good home and the companionship of pals it gradually got unbearable. I did not stay in a better hotel for certain obvious reasons. I do not like the hangers-on who come up to you and start talking just because they recognise your photograph in a newspaper. I do not like dressing up for meals and I like to be left alone when I want to be left alone.

But in Gallarate, it was finally a question of getting out or going mad with boredom. I even had to use the public baths as there were not any in the hotel. I used to put off getting up in the morning until as late as possible so that the days when we were not actually testing at the MV factory were not too long. I would have a light breakfast and go back to my room to write letters or read – and Tarzan comics or a who-dun-it thriller was about the limit of reading matter on offer. I found myself going down to the factory every morning and afternoon just to see if there was any mail from home – or from anywhere. Although some other riders would no doubt have made much more of their leisure in Italy, to me life was dragging along from one weekend to the next when I would be expected to switch suddenly from being a rather homesick Rhodesian to a speed-crazy devil in a leather suit.

The weekend after the TT races I rode at Mallory Park and then it was back to Italy. The following weekend I was due to ride in San Remo and as we were preparing to travel I heard I was not being sent. The bike, said Count Agusta, needed working on and was not fit to race.

And that did it!

Maybe it was the culmination of months of the Italian mentality of 'domain' when everything can be clarified tomorrow. Maybe it was the anti-climax after the TT races. Maybe it was the thought of the number of top riders killing themselves. I think it was all of that, plus the questions I found myself asking all the time – is it worth it and where do we go from here?

Just before the TT races, my country's government had given me a great honour when I was awarded the MBE in the Queen's Birthday Honours List. Somehow, sitting in that small room in the Italian hotel it all seemed so unreal and without thinking my request would even be considered, let alone agreed, I wrote to Count Agusta asking to be released from the rest of my contract which was due to expire at the end of the current season.

I spoke later that day to the boss and he agreed to release me. We discussed the financial implications and came to a mutual understanding. Within a few hours I had booked myself a seat home on the following day's plane from Rome. It all happened as quickly as that. Today in Bulawayo, I am as happy as a lark and plan to start working for myself pretty soon.

Maybe one day I will give car racing a go, for I have always had an urge to switch from two wheels to four. But at the moment if I ever swing my leg over a saddle again, it will be purely for fun and I spend much of my time these days turning down requests to ride somewhere in Southern Africa. I only hope I can stay out of the sport which has given me so much. I hope my will-power is enough to prevent me crawling back, for I have had my fill of the big time thrills.

I do not really know where I am heading or what I want out of life, other than to be allowed to live a natural existence, marry one day, have kids and settle down in

Bulawayo. On the map you may not even find the little Southern Rhodesian city with its 50,000 inhabitants, but to me it is home and my contentedness (if there is such a word) these days is because I am among my own pals and I can be myself instead of a Jekyll and Hyde with no real home and a pile of discarded Tarzan comics.

Why should I need to add anything to that? It tells us exactly what he was thinking, what he decided to do, and why he did it. I feel it would only be disrespectful to Gary to add anything. Speaking to *Motorcycle News* a few weeks later, Gary did reiterate that the death of his friend had nothing to do with his decision. "Directly it had nothing to do with the death of Tom Phillis at the TT races. A lot of people have said that his death affected me deeply and that I lost my nerve. But trying to put my thoughts into some sort of chronological order, the Phillis tragedy was not even the last straw. It certainly helped to put my thinking into focus, but I had done a great deal of thinking before the TT," he said, just as he wrote in the letter, before going into how miserable and lonely he was in the small hotel in Italy with time on his hands.

I will pick up on three points. Gary wrote that he and Count Agusta came to "a mutual understanding." He was prepared to repay Agusta any penalties he would meet by withdrawing from his contract early, but the Count generously said he would pay Gary the remainder of his contract.

Second, he said that there had been persistent rumours that he was going to get married. And third, near the end, he doesn't rule out the possibility that maybe one day he would give car racing a go.

10
Life without bikes

GARY HOCKING WAS a hero in Rhodesia and South Africa. He was honoured with the title of Rhodesian Sportsman of the year in 1959, and again in his championship-winning year of 1961. When he returned as champion, the reception was akin to that which royalty might receive. He was the main attraction every time he sat on a motorcycle; people came out to watch him race, and watch him win. He attracted huge crowds wherever he went.

He was particularly loved in his hometown of Bulawayo, and the town greeted him with a welcome worthy of their most famous son. Fame had come the way of Gary Hocking, but it hadn't altered how he remembered his friends, and those who had supported him on his way to stardom. He had purchased a modest house in the suburbs of Bulawayo, and had no interest in fancy cars or the high life.

Going home meant more to Gary than the city – he was returning to his long-time girlfriend, Valerie Chorley, who knew him as well as, if not better than, most.

The two had met at Saturday afternoon movies back in 1958, when they were introduced by friends. As with his life on the bikes, Gary, as Val recalls, was quick off the mark. "I was there with girlfriends; he was there with his friends," said Val. "We ended up going out on a date that night! I can't recall whether I knew that Gary was famous, or popular, or renowned for anything at that time, but I recall that he had a wonderful sense of humour; he was fun to be around."

So was it love at first sight? "Oh no," said Valerie, but then continued: "As a woman you think 'What does he see in me?' I don't know and I still don't know, it was just one of those things, we got on well together."

When I asked if she found him attractive, Val responded very quickly. "Well you've seen the pictures, he was very attractive, of course he was. He was good-looking and good-natured. The thing about Gary was that he was adored by men as well as women, I don't think anyone met Gary and disliked him. He was most likeable and modest."

It is not only Val Chorley who has said this about Gary Hocking. Everyone I have spoken to about Sox has said exactly the same – no-one has a bad word to say about him, and in the competitive nature of the business he was in, that is quite remarkable.

Valerie continued by asserting that fame never altered Gary, "he never came over as a big deal, never ever, even at the height of his fame in Bulawayo, he was just the same old Sox, although I never called him Sox, I always called him Gary."

Val might have thought Gary was good-looking, but photographs of Val show that she was something of a catch as well, and Gary made sure he looked after the girl on his arm. "I was very young at the time, and he would take me to visit John Wells and his wife, Maureen, and I was quite the frightened young girl as all these people seemed so grown up, but Gary was so protective and loving."

Returning to South Africa meant serious work for Hocking. Most weekends there would be races to attend, and between the dates on the track work would have to be done to get the machines ready, but still, as Val remembers, there was time for fun. "Gary and I were like two big kids, really. There was a tractor tyre at Jim Redman's place, and I remember the two of us curling up inside the tractor tyre and rolling down the hill; those were the sort of things we got up to."

Val rarely went to races with Gary unless they were local – certainly, she never travelled to Europe with him – but there was one instance when she travelled with him and Jim Redman. She recalls that they often stayed with friends, but on this occasion Gary gave her the 'star' treatment. "We were in the back of the van with Jim Redman, and the bikes: you can't believe this," she said, "we took it in turns to sleep on a row of petrol cans between the two bikes as we travelled along."

Things did get better. In Durban they would stay with Jim and Marlene Redman, and Paddy and Janet Driver would also stay there. There were other friends who would be pleased to see the riders and their wives or girlfriends, and provide accommodation. Val recalls one particular friend of Gary's called Ticky, but can't remember where he lived. She said Gary adored this guy.

Gary had moved in with the Chorley family, as Val recalls, but that didn't mean that she saw much more of him. "My young brother was at boarding school, and Gary, who was living with us, took my brother's bedroom. I remember he worked long hours in the garage at home, hammering out the metal fairing for the AJS. He made this thing and then had it made into fibreglass. That was really successful; he took that bike racing and he did brilliantly with it and went all over South Africa."

Even Hocking's favourite pastime involved motorbikes. Val recalls he loved scrambling, and she would go along and watch him. There were a few pastimes that didn't involve bikes, Val recalls: "He loved his music, but I never ever saw him play an instrument." One of his favourite groups was The Swingle Singers, one of whose earliest hits became the theme tune for a popular Italian television programme. Another favourite track, according to Val, was *Ain't Misbehavin'*, which about this time would have been sung by Louis Armstrong, although Jonnie Ray's version did make the UK charts in 1959.

Once Hocking travelled to Europe, his relationship with Val continued from a distance, but she was never worried about losing her man. This was the time, of course, before emails and other social media that we now take for granted, so contact was by the good old-fashioned letter. Val said that she was never concerned about what Gary was up to. He would be going to events around the motorbike races and no-doubt meeting girls, but on the other hand she was still going out with her friends and meeting people, too. Jim Redman recalled that Gary found it difficult to get girlfriends, which is something of a surprise looking at his photographs. Redman thinks that he didn't want to commit himself enough. "He was holding back and didn't want to get serious and all that." There was a time, recalled Val, when plans were discussed about setting up a place in Europe. "He told me that he and Jim [Redman] had talked about setting Marlene and me up in Switzerland but that never happened, as it came when he decided to drop the bikes and concentrate on cars."

Despite his close relationship with Valerie, Gary seldom, if ever, talked about his races. She said "he either won them or he didn't." As for other riders, it was a similar policy, and certainly friendships or dislikes he had with other riders never became a topic of conversation. Having said that, his dislike of Mike Hailwood was never discussed. Val could see a marked difference between the two MV riders. "Mike Hailwood was an entirely different personality to the type of person Gary was. Gary had more integrity and respect I would think. I know Mike is a hero in this country [the UK]."

Once he had some money in his pocket, Sox was able to buy himself a new car. Val said "he hated it, and only had it for a very short while before getting rid of it and buying an old Chevrolet van from the early '50s. Gary and a very good friend, Ray Murray, worked for hours every night on this old van just as he did with his bikes. Everyone in Bulawayo knew that old fawn Chevrolet van, and knew that if you saw it, it was Gary Hocking. So if you went out with Gary you were taken out in an old Chevy van! As a crowd we would all go out to Matopos for huge picnics, and Gary would pile all the kids into the car and just drive through the bush, and I mean *through* the bush, and take these kids and they loved it."

There is one other amusing story relating to the famous Chevy, recalled by Sean Robinson. When Gary arrived back in Bulawayo as world champion in 1961, he received a tumultuous welcome from crowds of people, but also received a reception from the dignitaries of Bulawayo. It was best bib and tucker time – something of a rarity for Gary, who was driving to the City Hall when the Chevy broke down. Luckily, following close behind was Sean Robinson, who attached the broken down vehicle to his own and began to tow Gary to the city centre. A little distance away they pulled up, as Gary thought it was a bit of a comedown to be arriving at a civic reception in a broken down van being towed!

Val didn't know anything about this, as she was already inside City Hall being entertained by the Mayor Jack Paine. "I had to meet him beforehand, and he took me to the Bulawayo Club and said to go with him to somewhere no woman had ever been before. He grabbed my hand and he was rather like a naughty little boy as we ran through, and he said 'There you are, you have just been where no woman has ever been before.'" Val recalls that Gary met the Mayor and there were lots of photographs, it being "something of a big deal."

Gary had learnt to speak fluent Italian whilst in Italy, and could converse easily with the Italian mechanics, but Val noticed that his wardrobe had improved as well. "He had some beautiful clothes, which he had never had before – you know what Italians dress like, really nice shoes and smart jackets and beautifully tailored suits. All these things which he had never had before, so that when the occasion arose Gary could really dress up. It was so nice for him; happy days."

Remembering other times they had together Val recalled that "he taught me to drive as well at Heany. It was in a little [Ford] Prefect that he bought for me, and I paid him back every month. There was never a big thing, 'I'm a big deal I'll give you this.' It was here you are learn to drive and you pay me back every month."

You do get the impression from talking to Valerie that Gary could have snapped his fingers and just about any girl would have come running, but that wasn't the man. He tended to shield her from the dangers of his profession, although as she recalled, there was one race she went to where Gary had a spill, but thankfully wasn't hurt – "That was scary." He was obviously aware that at the end of the '50s and beginning of the '60s morals were very different to what they are today. Gary was anxious that people didn't look at Valerie and think that she was just a girl after someone attractive and good at his sport. "He was very protective of my reputation. He protected me from anyone thinking the wrong thing about us as a couple. He was that sort of man, and absolutely just a lovely person."

Despite his attempts to shield her from the dangers of riding bikes at the speed at which he did, Val admitted that she was worried about him. "I would never have persuaded him to stop. When somebody loves something like that you live with it, you go with it." Having said that, he never discussed other riders or his races with Val. She said there were times when Gary thought about the dangers and the consequences: "He would look at photos and say 'This photo here, these other three are dead.' He would look at photographs of close friends who had died, like Dicky Dale, and wonder what he was doing, and that is what made him go into cars, as he thought that was the safer option."

So when Gary made the decision to retire from motorcycle racing, was that a great relief to Val? After a pause of fully ten seconds she replied: "No. He was still racing. Was I happy about him racing cars? Well I thought like him that it was probably safer."

At one time Gary had no desire to switch from two wheels to four, but as early as March 1962, during a conversation with John Wells, he admitted that he was becoming bored and frustrated with motorbikes, and was considering going into cars. Later that year at the Isle of Man TT he had a conversation with Mick Woollett, during which he confessed to the frustration of his lifestyle, the lack of races he was experiencing with MV, and the thoughts he had about quitting. He had one last desire though, and that was to win the big one at the TT. By the time he put his thoughts about retiring from motorcycle racing down on paper, he was obviously giving cars consideration. By August 1962, Gary had borrowed a car and won his first ever race at Marlborough track in Salisbury. He was close friends with Paddy Driver, who had made the switch from two wheels to four, and sought his advice on how to get himself into a car. Driver was a great friend of Reg Parnell, who following the Second World War had become team manager for the Bowmaker-Yeoman Racing Team, which had John Surtees as one of its drivers. Hocking decided this was the future, and sought the advice of Parnell in England with an introduction from Driver.

Reg's son, Tim Parnell, was selling a car at the time, and he said that Hocking came to look at it in Derby and wanted his father's advice. "He was desperate to get to know my father and further his career with him." Tim was also a driver, but had been forced out of racing in 1962 due to injury. Having seen what John Surtees had done in a car following a sparkling motorcycle career, Parnell senior seemed to think that Hocking was cut from the same cloth, and offered him a drive in his son's Lotus. "The problem was," said Parnell, "my father had John Surtees and his Lola in his team. Surtees wouldn't allow any relationship with Hocking. He was very jealous, and it made things very difficult for my father to do anything for Gary."

The car, a four-cylinder 18/21, was outdated by then-modern standards in the V8 era, but it would be good enough to give Gary the drives he was craving. His first drive came in England at Mallory Park at the August Bank Holiday meeting. Out-of-date machinery or not, it made little difference to Hocking, who qualified for his first ever race in the car and put it on pole position. As quick out of the blocks in a car as he was on a bike, Gary led for the first three laps until he was overtaken by the eventual winner Brian Hart. In trying to regain the lead, Hocking got into a spin thanks to the appalling conditions. That put him back to third, when he was involved in a dice with third-placed Chris Summers. The pressure was too much for the engine of the Lotus and he was forced out of the race, which some say he could have won. Tim Parnell said "he had a terrific drive in it. He was right up there with the leaders, and impressed everyone with his driving there."

Reg Parnell knew that, as well as Surtees, he had another driver of exceptional ability on his books, and entered him in the same car for the Danish Grand Prix at Roskildering. This race, a non-championship event run to Formula One rules, was new territory for Gary, who, with an out-of-date car, stood little chance of winning against the V8s. It consisted of three heats: one of 20 laps run on the Saturday and two of 30 the following day.

Starting seventh on the grid, just two seconds behind Jack Brabham on pole, Hocking finished eighth in the first two heats and fourth in the final heat on the Sunday. His aggregate position was fourth in a time of 1 hour 1 minute 35.4 seconds, which was 2 minutes 20 seconds behind winner Brabham.

He was the fastest driver of a four-cylinder machine, and at the start of the second heat had a real tussle with one of the top drivers of the time, Roy Salvadori – one of Reg Parnell's Bowmaker team. *Autosport* of August 31st 1962 reported that "Roy Salvadori went out of the race on the first lap when he became involved with Gary Hocking, in the Lotus he has brought from Tim Parnell, and Ian Burgess, both of whom could continue." In the final heat, again won by Brabham, *The Autocar* reports: "Fourth place, after a magnificent drive, went to Gary Hocking's four-cylinder car."

Next step for Gary was to enter the Gold Cup at Oulton Park the first week in September. Hocking took up 11th position on the grid, but was the fastest four-cylinder car amongst the starters. Drivers such as Jim Clark, Graham Hill, Bruce McLaren, Brabham, Surtees, Salvadori and Ireland were all in front of him in their more modern V8 machines. He stuck with them for the first lap, but his temperature gauge started to rise, and a two-minute pit stop cost him several places. He fought his way back to lead the four-cylinder machines until an oil pipe broke and his race ended on the 63rd lap of the 73. He was heading for a fifth place finish before his withdrawal, but had done enough for people to take notice of his achievement. In his article in *Autosport* magazine, McLaren wrote that Hocking was a "coming man."

"There was so much talent there," added Parnell. "The only thing that concerned me was that he was fearless. He admitted afterwards to me the things that he had done shook him; the risks that he had taken." Parnell, though, had no doubt that Hocking would have been a force in Formula One racing, "without a doubt. He was a terrific chap and there is no doubt about it – Gary Hocking would have been a top Formula One driver."

Hocking brought the Lotus from Tim Parnell, who thinks he must have paid something in the region of two or three thousand pounds for it, and, just as with motorcycle racing when the season in Europe was ending, so the season in South Africa was beginning. Gary Hocking, and his Lotus were on the way to Bulawayo.

When he returned home, Hocking as usual met up with John Wells, and told him that the racing game was easy. "You have extra thinking time," he explained. "On a motorcycle if a bug smacks into the windshield it is right in front of your eyes. In a car you pick up the bug at the nose of the car and follow it right up the bonnet, then it hits the windscreen. There is so much more thinking time, it is so much easier."

The Gold Star series featured several drivers who had been successful in Europe, including John Love, Tony Maggs, and Bruce Johnstone. The first event Gary entered was the Rand Spring Trophy on October 10th. It was the first of two races that would give drivers the chance to prepare for the South African Grand Prix in December, and although a good number of the big names hadn't arrived, Hocking thrashed the opposition on offer. He took pole position from practice, and regularly broke the lap record as he won both the 24-lap heats, with the recorded time of 1 hour 19 minutes 39.7 seconds at an average of 91.8mph. The Total Cup, a minor meeting at Zwartkops, was a similar story.

There was great excitement leading up to the 2nd December, when the Rhodesian Grand Prix would be held in Bulawayo for the first time. It was a "heyday for the city," reported *The Bulawayo Chronicle*, and as there would be the usual mix of cars and bikes, they were pleased to welcome 'home' not only Gary Hocking, but Jim Redman as well, in the "finest line-up of drivers and motorcyclists ever seen in Bulawayo"

The morning after the race, *The Bulawayo Chronicle* celebrated Gary's win as its lead story. "Great Grand Prix win by Hocking," was the headline. "He beats the lap record 36 (yes 36!) times," wrote *Checkpoint*.

The praise continued: "Gary Hocking proved himself to be Rhodesia's greatest ever motor sportsman at Kumalo track yesterday when he tar-scorched his way for 50 laps to win the Rhodesian Grand Prix." *Checkpoint* called the drive "faultless," and added that apart from the 36-lap records in the Grand Prix, he also broke the lap record in the Formula Libre race another nine times.

So, Gary now held the lap records at Kumalo in cars and on bikes. Explaining why his race laps were two seconds slower than in practice, he told a reporter "you have to take it more carefully in the race. If you spun off you are out of the race."

The extremely hot weather must have taken its toll on the cars, as only half the 14 starters finished the race. The only disappointment for those watching was that the eagerly anticipated contest between Hocking and the first South African to ever appear in a world championship table, Tony Maggs, never materialised, because Maggs was one of those forced out of the race with mechanical trouble. He was, though, apparently the first to congratulate Gary on his win. Hocking was becoming as successful on four wheels as he was on two, and his rise was as rapid.

11

The final lap

J UST AS GARY had received help launching his career on bikes, so he found a mentor who believed in his ability in cars: Reg Parnell. Parnell could see that the Lotus was holding back Hocking, and he needed to get amongst the V8s, which Parnell couldn't provide at that time. Also there was the problem with Surtees, who would not have any relationship with Hocking whatsoever. So Parnell contacted Rob Walker and asked him to put Gary into the Lotus 24 in the bigger races on the horizon in South Africa.

Rob Walker was heir to the Johnny Walker whisky fortune, so had the financial ability to launch his own Grand Prix motor racing team in 1953. He made a few appearances himself as a driver, but his main claim to fame had been through his Lotus team. As Gary Hocking was making a name for himself as a driver of cars for Reg Parnell, so Walker had a vacancy in his team because Stirling Moss had been involved in a major crash at Goodwood – one that would end his career. Also, Ricardo Rodriguez had been involved in a fatal crash in the Mexican Grand Prix in November. Walker was looking out for the next Stirling Moss, and Parnell thought he might have found just the man – that is how highly Gary Hocking was regarded, even this early into his car racing career. Tim Parnell said: "My father spoke to Rob Walker and said, 'Sign this lad up, he's going to be a future champion.'"

A deal was done and letters were exchanged. The first came on the headed notepaper from the RRC Walker Racing team at Pipbrook Garage, London Road, Dorking, and dated 31st October 1962. The letter was sent to Gary at Upton Road, Queens Park East in Bulawayo, and started Dear Gary Hocking. Walker expressed his delight that Hocking would be driving for him in South Africa next year, and looked forward to a very happy and successful partnership.

Walker continued by saying that they were having difficulty in getting the cars back from Mexico in time to get to Africa for December 10th. The cars, he explained, had to go to England to be prepared before then being shipped to

Africa. Gary was asked whether he preferred to have a five- or six-speed gearbox, it being suggested that the six-speed box was new and still rather suspect, whereas the five-speed was well proven.

Walker further explained that, for next year, he wasn't certain about the makeup of the cars, as Coventry Climax – which provided the engines – was dropping out of racing, but that he had been offered BMW engines, and hoped to get hold of the chassis used by Graham Hill that year. Walker was confident that they would have something at least fairly good for Gary to drive.

The letter ended with Walker congratulating Gary on his excellent drives in the Rand GP, and wishing him all the best for the South African races. Walker hoped to meet Gary at the South African Grand Prix, and he was sending out a mechanic with the car.

On November 5th, Gary replied that he was pleased to receive the letter of 31st October, which was the first confirmation he had that he had been signed for the Walker team. He said that he had studied the dates of the races and the shipping dates, and was suggesting that the car be sent on the *Edinburgh Castle* to Durban, which was eight hours' drive from Johannesburg, where the first South African race was taking place on December 15th.

He expressed a wish to have the five-speed gearbox, as he had one on his present car and found it quite suitable. He was interested in the BMW engine, but, concerning the chassis, felt the Lotus was better, and he looked forward to meeting Rob Walker in East London. Signed, Gary Hocking.

The next communication was dated 9th November, and was signed by Rob Walker's secretary, Miss VA Wilkin. She confirmed that a space had been reserved on the *Edinburgh Castle* sailing from London on 22nd November, but rather than go to Durban she suggested the car be offloaded at Cape Town, as even with a drive of 1000 miles the cars could be in Johannesburg before the ship docked in Durban. She implied that all of the changes in plans were due to the return of the cars from Mexico, where they believe in 'mañana!'

On 14th November Rob Walker wrote to Gary again, confirming that the car would be sailing on the *Edinburgh Castle*, leaving on the 22nd for Cape Town. He was writing the day before the car was due back in England from Mexico, which he said would give them very little time to do much preparation, but not to worry, as the engines could do three Grands Prix without servicing. Walker was pleased that Gary had chosen the five-speed gearbox, as the car with the six-speed had been written-off in Mexico. Walker ended his letter with a plea to Gary. "Take it carefully in your first race," he wrote. "I think it would be best to get used to the car, and you have plenty of time to do that, and if you are not up amongst the leaders I shall not worry at all, because I have perfect confidence in your capabilities and would far rather you took it gently to start with and got the feel of the car."

Walker finished by hoping all went well in the first races, and said he was looking forward to seeing Gary in East London.

29th November Walker wrote again, confirming the car had left on the *Edinburgh Castle*, and that arrangements had been made to take it up to Johannesburg. He confirmed that the car had arrived from Mexico in time for them to strip the chassis "and replace everything that needed it." The engine had been sent back to Climax, where the big ends had been replaced, the head was lifted, and everything was alright for the moment, but Climax was implying that the bearings would only do one race at a time without replacement.

Walker said that he was sending his mechanic, Tony Cleverley, to Johannesburg with enough spares to service the engine after each race. "Even though he is quite young he has been racing with me for about five years, and has managed to look after Stirling on his own. I think you will find him very nice, willing and competent," said Walker.

Gary replied on December 4th, saying that he was pleased that the car was on its way. He said that he would be staying in 'Jo'burg,' and would contact Mr Cleverley there. Gary continued that, as for next year, "I think I would like to leave the choice of machinery completely up to you as I have very little experience in these matters." He finished by saying that he would wire Rob Walker with the results from Jo'burg immediately after the race.

The car, the mechanic, Tony Cleverley, and Gary were all together in time for the Rand Grand Prix in Kyalami. Gary qualified in 11th place, 4.3 seconds behind the driver on pole position, Jim Clarke. This was the first chance Cleverley had to watch Hocking in the car, but he was impressed. "He was pretty quick," said Cleverley, "he was a good quick driver. There was one thing I would say about him, at Kyalami I had to put out a signal board to him to stay on the track because he kept dropping a couple of wheels off the track and onto the dirt. He was going quick even at the first race, which I liked because I thought 'At least he is trying.'"

It was Hocking's first taste of the V8's power in the Lotus 24, but he was unhappy with its handling. Despite this, he stuck to the tail of the winner, Jim Clark, second-placed Trevor Taylor, and his old rival from his motorcycle days, John Surtees. Hocking was lapped by the first three, but had the honour of being the first local rider to finish. His lap speed in the V8 had been 2.5 seconds slower than his laps in the Lotus 18/21.

Two weeks after the Rand was the South African Grand Prix, and Hocking already had ambitions to mix it with the top drivers, who would be Clark and Graham Hill, but in the intervening week attention fell on Westmead and the Natal Grand Prix on December 22nd. The Lotus 24 went better at Westmead, although Gary had thought about reverting to the tried and tested 18/21, and he put in a practice time on his first attempt of 1 minute 25.1 seconds, which would have made him third fastest, and placed him on the front row of the grid. Despite having a good time under his belt, Gary decided to practise further. Tony Cleverley said he didn't need to, but he simply wanted more time in the car. It proved to be a fatal decision. As he was approaching a corner known as the Devil's Leap, his car spun off the track.

Fifteen-year-old Rennie Mackrory was due to be working on one of the gates and was walking around to his allotted point. "The track was a little above us and to the left of me," he said. "There was the screaming of an engine, and the Lotus 24 suddenly appeared in front of us and somersaulted end over end and then disappeared out of sight." Mackrory added that other people had seen Gary come up what was known as the Rise, and at this point the track went into a bit of a cutting. They said that as he was coming up the Rise, he appeared to get a couple of wheels on the dirt. The car suddenly shot off to the left, which they said indicated a suspension failure or something, and that is what launched the car into the air. When Mackrory saw the car he estimated it was about 20 feet in the air going end over end and the engine was screaming. He continued: "This must have been about 30 to 50 metres away from me, and I was shaking with fright. It was a hell of a shock."

The section of the track was on a gentle curve, but almost straight at the point of the accident, and must have been about 100 yards before the corner. It appears that just where the car landed, unlike today where there would be a considerable distance between the track and any obstructions, trees had recently been cut down, but the stumps had been left in the ground. Needless to say, the car was wrecked. In the words of Tony Cleverley, "I thought it was pretty well stuffed." He was in the pits at the time, and can't recall how far that was from the accident, but he added that he couldn't have just run out onto the track as practice was still going on. Rennie Mackrory recalls that it must have taken the marshals a good five minutes to get to Gary, who was removed from the wreckage still alive, but died on his way to the Addlington Hospital in Durban.

It was four days before Christmas, and back in Bulawayo girlfriend Val was shopping. "I was looking for Gary's Christmas present when one of my dear friends Milly Huckle rushed up and said come with me to *The Bulawayo Chronicle*, come with me, come with me now. That was the start, they told me that Gary had been killed. It was horrible, no-one would look at me, no-one would talk to me as they were all trying to avoid talking about it." They went to the *Chronicle* offices, as that would have been the place where news of the accident was coming in. She asked if he was badly injured, only to be told he had died. She was due to pick up her mother, so "I had to get myself together and go back to my car and drive to where I was due to pick her up." Her father was waiting at their home to break the news to her gently, but was beaten to the task by the sheer weight of the story and the reaction it prompted. "Everywhere I was, people were putting their heads out of car windows and saying how sorry they were hearing about Gary and crying. It was like walking through glue," she added.

The whole of Bulawayo was in mourning over the death of one of its heroes. The following day, *The Bulawayo Chronicle* gave over the whole of its front page to Gary's death. "Gary Hocking killed in car crash," was the headline. "Death at Devil's Leap in 90mph double turnover." The article reported that the news of

Hocking's death had "spread through Bulawayo like a grass fire." *The Chronicle* lines were jammed with anxious callers. Bulawayo was full of numbed citizens. There was a photograph of a smiling Hocking; another of him on a motorbike; the MV he had borrowed for the 1959 race at Kumalo; another of him in a car in the Rand Grand Prix, and one of him being presented with the Chronicle Cup at the start of the Rhodesian Grand Prix. From now on, the caption declared, it would be known as the Hocking Memorial Trophy. There was a picture of him with Val, and with his mother at the TT.

People – those who could speak – paid their tributes. Jim Redman was too numbed to say too much, John Wells was so upset he couldn't speak at all, but later said "I am choked. I thought Sox would never kill himself. We have lost one of the greatest sportsmen this country has ever produced." Tributes came from the Prime Minister of Southern Rhodesia, and from those who knew him from the local motor clubs. Even the RAC in England issued a statement, and the news was carried in several English newspapers and on the Isle of Man. In Newport, news was also received of Gary's death. His brother returned from work to find his parents sitting in their house, which at that time he thought was strange. They asked if he had heard the news, and when he was told he was naturally devastated.

At the inquest a misadventure verdict was recorded, but from that day speculation and theories have been submitted as to how the accident happened. Redman has the theory that Hocking blacked out through dehydration. "Gary never used to like to sweat," remembered the six-time world champion. "We would be drinking water like mad before a race and when we had our leathers on we would sweat. Gary never drank water or anything else, and I think he blacked out and went off the road. One thing is for certain Gary would not have made a mistake approaching that bend, he didn't make those sort of mistakes." At the enquiry held after the tragedy, the doctor who examined Gary said that he had been dehydrated, and Redman's theory is further supported by the fact that there were no skid marks on the track. If there had been a mechanical failure, the driver would have applied the brakes and there would be skid marks.

Others have suggested that the suspension on the car broke. The throttle cable ran through the pipes or was attached to the suspension, and when the chassis gave way it caused the throttle cable to be pulled down, making the car increase speed, and there was nothing Gary could do to stop it. Remember the account of the witness Rennie Mackrory, who said "there was this screaming of engines." Mackrory continued: "Friends of mine watched Gary come up the hill, and it appeared that he got two wheels on the dirt." It seemed that Gary was prone to letting the car drift onto the dirt or stones at the side of the tarmac. Tony As Cleverley recalled: "At Kyalami I had to put a signal board out to him to stay on the track because he kept dropping a couple of wheels off the track and onto the dirt." Another witness told the inquest that he thought Hocking had driven too fast and too wide into the corner.

Two well-known and very experienced mechanics, Fred Goddard and Ray Read, later examined the car. They were both convinced that the cause of the accident was a chassis failure. It appeared that the chassis had received a lot of welding, and those welds had failed at the critical moment.

The Lotus 24 also had a history of steering failure. A year after Hocking's accident, Paddy Driver, who also converted from bikes to cars, was trying to qualify for the South African Grand Prix when he actually saw the steering arm of his car drop after he had gone over a bump. His car left the road and flipped over. Luckily, Driver survived the experience, but after hearing eyewitness reports he was convinced that a similar fate befell Gary Hocking's car. Gary had already qualified on the front row of the grid for the Natal Grand Prix, so he didn't have to go for a faster time. Tony Cleverley said that he was simply going out again to get used to the car and the circuit.

Whatever the cause of the accident, the result would not be the same in modern day Formula One. On a modern race track, Hocking would have travelled onto the huge run-off areas that surround the circuits, and even if he had overshot these he would have come up against a soft barrier. At Westmead things were very different – the run-off was littered with the stumps of trees that had recently been cut down, and a flimsy Formula One car offered little to protect the driver. An ambulance did eventually arrive at the scene, although it took some time for witnesses to inform the authorities that there had been an accident.

Sometime after the crash, Gary's helmet and driving gear were sent to his parents' house in Newport. Duncan said that you could see where the roll bar at the back of the seat had cut right through his helmet and smashed his skull.

The day after his death, the Prime Minister of Rhodesia sent a personally signed letter to Mrs Hocking saying how very distressed he was to hear of Gary's death. He wrote: "Gary was truly one of the world's great sportsmen, and his outstanding contribution to Rhodesian sport will long be remembered."

Such was the esteem with which Gary Hocking was held in Rhodesia, over 300 people turned up for a memorial service in Bulawayo. However, his parents asked for his body to be returned to Wales. He was buried in Christchurch Cemetery, Newport on January 2nd 1963, a cold winter's day. The *South Wales Argus* reported that "Racing driver Gary Hocking was buried at his native Newport, two days after his body was flown home from South Africa. Sponsor and racing car owner Rob Walker was among the group of relatives at the graveside." Walker paid this tribute: "He was a truly great motorcyclist and would have undoubtedly been amongst the world's best racing drivers."

There was a representative from the Rhodesian and Nyasaland High Commission, and wreaths from neighbours, the Newport Car Club, Rhodesian Motor Sports Association, Bulawayo Motor Club, and the Matabeleland Car Club.

After being able to compose himself and put words on paper, John Wells wrote a tribute for Rhodesian national television, which is reproduced on page 164.

12

The legacy

JOHN SURTEES IS the only man to become world champion on both two wheels and four. He achieved that honour in 1964, when he won the Formula One world championship driving for Ferrari. Whilst John is very proud to be the only man to be a champion in both sports, he knows he will always be the first. But listening to people who know the sport of motor racing, might Gary Hocking have eventually been the first to have achieved that honour?

His rise was remarkable. From riding a motorcycle to work to becoming world champion on the 350cc and 500ccs took him four years. Given the speed at which he took to racing cars and the success he had in four months, coupled with the backing he received from first of all Reg Parnell and later Rob Walker, who knows? But for the accident which cost him his life, he might have beaten Surtees to the double championship.

Many world champions have left their mark on motorsport: Surtees, Hailwood, Redman, Duke, and more recently the likes of Barry Sheene and Carl Foggarty. But considering the short career Gary Hocking enjoyed, his legacy is quite remarkable.

The 300 people attending a memorial service for Gary in St John's Cathedral, Bulawayo, included the Mayor and city councillors, and representatives from the government. In his address, the acting rector, Reverand CW Stromberg, said: "We are here to remember a person who achieved fame and honour. His achievements will long be remembered." A collection at the end of the service donated £40 to the Gary Hocking Memorial Fund.

The fund, which opened a few days before the memorial service, was sponsored by the Rhodesian Motor Sports Association. Its purpose was to assist racing drivers, riders, and officials to meet expenses caused by injuries received during racing or practice. Letters had been sent around the world to motor racing journals, motor racing organisations in England, South Africa, and Australia.

The governing bodies of motorsport had also been invited to contribute. It was hoped to raise about £3000 initially. Much later, in January 1966, a letter from the chairman of the Gary Hocking Memorial Scholarship fund was sent to Arthur Hocking stating that a constitution had been approved, and naming several well-known businesses who had promised contributions. Some of these included Dunlop, MV Agusta, Rhodesian Breweries, and the Lions Club of Bulawayo.

The letter informed Arthur that the fund intended to provide a £300 a year scholarship for a four-year university course in engineering, but as yet they were well short of their target. The letter concluded by stating that "Gary was a most popular figure in Rhodesia and the esteem in which he was held is reflected in the encouraging support which his Memorial Fund is receiving."

The popularity of Gary Hocking led to several beneficiaries in Rhodesia, but away from the tributes and schemes to perpetuat his name there was a family who mourned a son, a brother, and of course Valerie, his girlfriend. She had no idea that he had stated he had no intention of going into cars, so for her the relief of him retiring from bikes never gave her any comfort. As she said, "he was still racing. Was I happy about him racing cars? Well like him I thought it was probably safer. He'd go into cars because it would be safer and he didn't want to be one of those numbers in the photographs. We never talked ever about a life when he wasn't racing," she continued.

For Val, it must have been harder than for anyone in Bulawayo. The Christmas she described as the worst ever, then followed the departure of the body back to Wales, and the memorial service early in January. Hocking was such a popular figure that there were bound to be people who felt the necessity to express their condolences. Kind as that might appear, it continually raises the memory. She escaped. "I saved up and went overseas to London. I had good friends there with me and everything was good." It was whilst she was in London that the friends she was staying with took her to South Wales and to Newport, to see Gary's grave. "That was like the final closure." Val also went to Gary's parents house, but they weren't at home, so as a result she was never able to meet them. "After two and a half years, when I felt everything was good, I went back to Rhodesia."

So would Valerie Chorley ever have become Valerie Hocking? Did she think he would ever ask, and what would she have said if he had? There was a resounding "Yes" from Val, who explained that, over the four years they had been together, the friendship had developed into love. "It was definitely a solid relationship, but I wouldn't guarantee that we would have got married, I was still very young at 22," she said. "We weren't going anywhere else than our relationship, but Gary had the world at his feet. He was so loved at home, so admired. Who knows? I don't know."

Valerie has moved on – she later married and had children – but talking to her you feel there are still some times in her life when she thinks back to Gary, the guy that he was, and what he achieved.

Back in South Wales, there was a family badly hit by the accident, and no matter what tributes were paid by friends or dignitaries from the highest level, they had lost a son and a brother. Duncan thinks that his father was the first one to get over the loss they had suffered. "We are talking about a couple who were raised through the Great Depression, and lived through the Second World War, and these were tough people, probably tougher than us. They didn't talk to me much about things. I do know that my mother took years to get her appetite back." As for Arthur, he called the family together and said that they must support each other to get through the tough times. "That was unusual," said Duncan. "That went on for a while."

The Hockings were asked where they wanted their son buried, and Arthur immediately said back home in Wales. They had seldom seen eye-to-eye, and Duncan recalls that his father didn't talk much about Gary and his motorcycle racing, though was immensely proud of his achievements.

Duncan Hocking admits that he probably felt the loss more than anyone. He returned home on the day the news broke of his brother's death, and recalls that it had been a strange day. "It seemed as though nobody [at work] was talking to me, I was almost in a bubble. I got home and both my parents were at home, which was strange as I always got home first. They asked had I heard the news, to which I replied what news, and they came straight out with it, 'Your brother has been killed in South Africa.'" Duncan continued, "I was affected probably more than they were, I had lost my hero."

The younger brother had contemplated going to help Gary with his racing, but it was decided he was too young. However, Duncan was determined that his brother's name would live on. "The only thing I could do," said Duncan, "was to do with bikes." After three years in the army, Duncan brought a Ducati and enrolled in the Charles Mortimer Racing School at Brands Hatch. He signed in as Mr Smith. Speaking at the time, Duncan said that he didn't want to disgrace the name of his brother. A problem came when he had to produce his driving licence, which, of course, was in the name of Duncan Hocking. It didn't take people long to put two and two together, and the word spread that "A new Hocking makes his bid."

Initial progress was good, but, come the races, Duncan spent more time sliding around on his leathers than riding around on the wheels. Everywhere he went he was tagged 'brother of the late Gary Hocking' – just what he didn't want. Friends, too, were concerned that his parents had suffered the trauma of losing one son through speed; why put them through the agony again?

Eric Davies, President of the Newport and Gwent Motorcycle Club, came up with the answer. He had been a sprinter, and suggested that Duncan, if he was determined to take part in motorsport, would do himself far less damage in a sprint than he would going around the racetracks. The seed sprouted and blossomed. Duncan became the best in the UK, and also tried his hand at drag racing, in which he also excelled, and was nominated as the best newcomer in his first year. Two years later, on a bike he designed, he broke world records, and became the best 750cc rider in the country.

A local company then approached Duncan with a view to sponsoring him, with the proviso that instead of sprinting he took up drag racing, as that was where the company generated most of its business. The success again came quickly. In one year he became the best British rider for 1973, and did demonstration races against the top American, Danny Johnson, in the International series at Santa Pod. Johnson invited Hocking to America to join his team – an invitation Duncan accepted, but unfortunately the bikes Johnson promised never materialised, and his career came to an end.

Does Duncan think he did justice to his brother's name? "Well, yes, because you can hardly see my name written without 'brother of the late Gary Hocking.'"

Out in South Africa, Hocking is remembered with displays of his memorabilia and trophies in the Historic Motorcycle Museum at the Lake Avenue Inn at Deneysville, just south of Johannesburg. Back in 2012, the 50th anniversary of his death, many of his friends gathered at Westmead to celebrate his achievements.

Near the former Westmead race track, which is now an industrial estate, his name lives on with many other greats of that era, as several roads and streets have been named after them, including Gary Hocking Place.

Daily Express motoring writer Basil Cardew wrote this of Gary: "He was considered by many experts to be the finest motorcyclist the world has known."

I go back to the beginning of this book and quote the former headmaster of Bulawayo Technical College, HJ Sutherby. He remembered the conversation with the teenager, and the line, "I want to become a racing motorcyclist, and I think I might make world class." Sutherby reflected in his letter to a national newspaper: "Today, I sat at a comfortable English fireside; the impassive television screen brought me the news of his death.

"We all know he made world class. Those who doubted his ability to do so he put to shame by the simple process of doing it."

Those who saw Gary Hocking race are now becoming fewer and fewer, as are those who had the undoubted pleasure of his company. In writing this book, I hope that his name will continue to be mentioned in motorcycling circles for a little longer.

Let's hope that Gary Hocking is no longer the forgotten champion.

A tribute

by John Wells

O F GARY HOCKING so much has been written and spoken that little remains to be added. He not only made history, but became a household name throughout the world. In his short career he won the admiration of millions all over the globe.

Gary grew up as any other Rhodesian boy. He was just the kid next door, but how he loved this sun-drenched country; even at the height of his career, any short period of free time found him rushing back to Bulawayo, for this was home. Although he had the world at his feet, he was happiest here.

To the many close friends that Gary Hocking had, he was known only as 'Sox,' the nickname that began in school days but was to follow him throughout his travels. In his normal, very casual form of dress he was just one of the boys, and his quiet unassuming way lost him to the crowd. He spoke freely of others, but his modest manner restricted any praise of his own many successes. He was heralded as supreme, illustrious, champion of champions bestowed with all the glory and honours that become a wonder boy, and yet he never altered from the days of Sox Hocking the unknown.

How well several of us recall the day Gary left on his first trip overseas to venture further afield in motor racing. On that cool early morning, he joined the passengers with a small suitcase containing all his material possessions, and, unlike his travelling companions, in his usual open-necked shirt. It was some three years later bringing with him a double world crown of motor cycling that he arrived to meet a much more dignified welcome home party, but still without his necktie. This indeed was Gary Hocking, who through sheer determination had become the fastest man on two wheels, but who never changed. The same attitude after his success won him his popularity: children loved him as their hero, adults admired him, many no-doubt envied his obvious gifted talents, but it was the short, sharp handshake of Gary Hocking that made one feel he was pleased to meet you again.

The name of this great motorcyclist will live a very long time. Perhaps he was the best ever, perhaps he will be bettered. To his friends, though, it was not only the loss of a great sportsman and world champion, but the absence of Sox himself, that left an empty feeling forever. Like so many others, I am left with a million memories, and an autographed photograph that reads simply:

"To John, thanks for everything – Sox."

Appendix

Gary Hocking results 1957-58, South Africa

Date	Machine	Venue	Race	Result
24/2/57	250cc Velocette	Salisbury	Geoff Duke International road race	1st 250cc scratch
4/4/57	350cc Norton	Salisbury	SMC & LCC National meeting	1st 350cc scratch
6/5/57	350cc Norton	Bulawayo	Heany 100 National meeting	1st 350cc scratch
31/5/57	350cc Norton	Pietermaritzburg	Union Day Races 350cc	1st 350cc scratch
	350cc Norton	Pietermaritzburg	Union Day Races 500cc	1st 500cc scratch
-/-/57	350cc Norton	Salisbury	MMCC National meeting	1st 350cc scratch
1/9/57	350cc Norton	Salisbury	Mashonland 100	1st 350cc scratch
12/10/57	350cc Norton	Johannesburg	International meeting	2nd behind Ken Robas
27/10/57	350cc Norton	Bulawayo	Heany Summer Handicap	1st 350cc scratch, 2nd Ken Robas
-/12/57	350cc Norton	Pietermaritzburg		1st 350cc scratch
1/1/58	350cc Norton	Port Elizabeth	PE 200	4th 350cc handicap
-/1/58	350cc Norton	Pietermaritzburg	National meeting	3rd 350cc scratch
20/4/58	650cc Triumph	Salisbury	International road race	2nd 500cc scratch
25/5/58	650cc Ridgeback	Bulawayo	Heany 100 National meeting	2nd 500cc scratch

Rides 1959-60, return to South Africa

Date	Machine	Venue	Race	Result
Oct 1959	Borrowed 250cc MV Agusta	New Kumalo circuit	Heany Summer Handicap	1st 250cc scratch
	Borrowed 500cc Norton	New Kumalo circuit	Heany Summer Handicap	1st 500cc scratch
Feb 1960	500cc Norton	Marlborough circuit, Salisbury	*Evening Standard* Trophy Road Races	1st 500cc scratch
Nov 1960	500cc MV Agusta	Kumalo circuit	National Road Races	1st 500cc scratch
Dec 1960	500cc MV Agusta	Belvedere circuit, Salisbury	National Road Races	1st 500cc Scratch
Dec 1960	500cc MV Agusta	East London	East London Grand Prix	4th 500cc scratch

Isle of Man TT results

Date	Event	Machine	Result
1959	Junior TT	350cc Norton	12th
1960	Ultra Lightweight	125cc MV Agusta	2nd
	Lightweight	250cc MV Agusta	1st
1961	Lightweight	250cc MV Agusta	Failed to finish
	Junior	350cc MV Agusta	2nd
	Senior	500cc MV Agusta	Failed to finish
1962	Junior	350cc MV Agusta	2nd
	Senior	500cc MV Agusta	1st

1961 Summer Series, South Africa, dates unknown

Venue	Event	Machine	Result
Zwartkop	350cc	350cc AJS 7R borrowed from Bruce Beal	1st
	500cc	350cc AJS 7R borrowed from Bruce Beal	3rd behind Phil Read and Paddy Driver
Kumalo	350cc scratch race	350cc AJS 7R borrowed from Bruce Beal	1st
	Star Riders Handicap	350cc AJS 7R borrowed from Bruce Beal	1st
Roy Hesketh	350cc Handicap race	On own 350cc AJS 7R	1st
	350cc scratch race	On own 350cc AJS 7R	1st
	500cc scratch race	On own 350cc AJS 7R	2nd behind Paddy Driver
Westmead	350cc scratch race	On own 350cc AJS 7R	1st
	500cc scratch race	On own 350cc AJS 7R	Failed to finish
East London	350cc scratch race	On own 350cc AJS 7R	1st
	500cc scratch race	On own 350cc AJS 7R	3rd behind Phil Read and Paddy Driver
Final meeting at Roy Hesketh cancelled.			

World championship races

Year	Machine	Race	Position	WC position
1958	500cc Norton	Dutch TT Assen	6th	
	500cc Norton	West German GP Nürburgring	3rd	
	500cc Norton	Swedish GP Hedemora	4th	6th
	125cc MZ	Ulster GP Dundrod Circuit	2nd	
	125cc MV Agusta	Nations GP Monza	6th	9th
1959	250cc MZ	Swedish GP Råbelöfsbanan	1st	
	250cc MZ	Ulster GP Dundrod Circuit	1st	2nd
	350cc Norton	French GP Charade Circuit	2nd	
	350cc Norton	Isle of Man TT	12th	
	350cc Norton	West German GP Hockenheim	2nd	4th
	500cc Norton	French GP Charade Circuit	3rd	
	500cc Norton	Belgian GP Spa	2nd	5th
1960	125cc MV Agusta	Isle of Man TT	2nd	
	125cc MV Agusta	Dutch TT Assen	2nd	
	125cc MV Agusta	Belgian GP Spa	5th	
	125cc MV Agusta	Ulster GP Dundrod Circuit	2nd	
	125cc MV Agusta	Nations GP Monza	5th	2nd
	250cc MV Agusta	Isle of Man TT	1st	
	250cc MV Agusta	Dutch TT Assen	2nd	
	250cc MV Agusta	Belgian GP Spa	2nd	
	250cc MV Agusta	West German GP Solitude	1st	2nd
	350cc MV Agusta	French GP Charade	1st	
	350cc MV Agusta	Dutch TT Assen	2nd	
	350cc MV Agusta	Nations GP Monza	1st	2nd
1961	250cc MV Agusta	Spanish GP Montjuïc circuit	1st	8th
	350cc MV Agusta	Isle of Man TT	2nd	
	350cc MV Agusta	Dutch TT Assen	1st	
	350cc MV Agusta	East German GP Sachsenring	1st	
	350cc MV Agusta	Ulster GP Dundrod	1st	
	350cc MV Agusta	Nations GP Monza	1st	1st

World championship races *continued* ...

Year	Machine	Race	Position	WC position
1961	500cc MV Agusta	West German GP Hockenheim	1st	
	500cc MV Agusta	French GP Charade	1st	
	500cc MV Agusta	Dutch TT Assen	1st	
	500cc MV Agusta	Belgian GP Spa	1st	
	500cc MV Agusta	East German GP Sachsenring	1st	
	500cc MV Agusta	Ulster GP Dundrod	1st	
	500cc MV Agusta	Swedish GP Kristianstad	1st	1st
1962	350cc MV Agusta	Isle of Man TT	2nd	8th
	500cc MV Agusta	Isle of Man TT	1st	5th

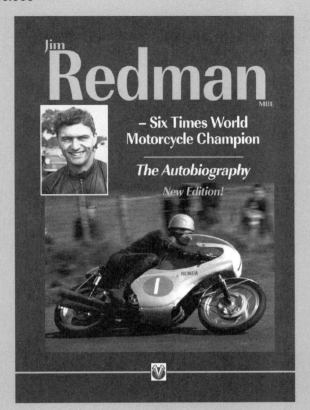

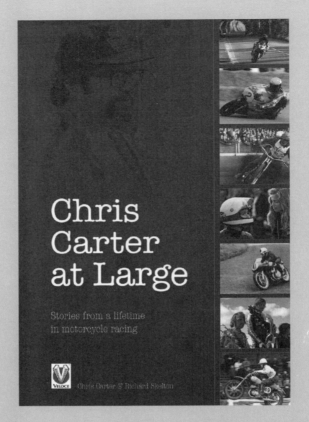

Chris Carter at Large

Stories from a lifetime
in motorcycle racing

VELOCE

Chris Carter & Richard Skelton

"For decades Chris Carter was a much-loved motorcycling journalist and
commentator, professions that demanded getting close to all the top stars ...
Anyone with motorcycle sport in his veins won't be able to put this book down
as Chris writes in an amazingly frank manner, with 'nowt left out' ... Chris – who
was helped considerably in the compilation of his book by Richard Skelton – has
produced a truly mighty winner, and it comes highly recommended."
– *Old Bike Mart*

ISBN: 978-1-845840-91-4
Paperback • 22.5x15.2cm • £16.99* UK/$29.95* USA • 240 pages • 100 pictures

For more info on Veloce titles, visit our website at www.veloce.co.uk
• email: info@veloce.co.uk • Tel: +44(0)1305 260068
* prices subject to change, p&p extra

"Lambert's perspective as a reporter of the action, third-party observer of the politics and processes and narrator of the triumph and tragedy that goes with the TT makes his book a compelling thing to read. It is part memoir revealing his close personal affinity for the place, the event and its people and part history, recalling with fascinating detail not only who won which event, but how."
– *Ultimate MotorCycling*

ISBN: 978-1-845847-50-0
Paperback • 22.5x15.2cm • £14.99* UK/$24.95* USA • 160 pages
• 45 colour pictures

For more info on Veloce titles, visit our website at www.veloce.co.uk
• email: info@veloce.co.uk • Tel: +44(0)1305 260068
* prices subject to change, p&p extra

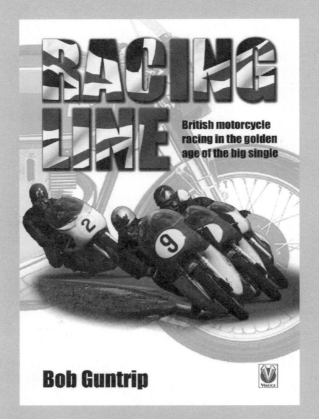

"I thoroughly enjoyed watching motocross and trials in the 1950s and 1960s and didn't bother with motorcycle racing, but Bob Guntrip's book has shown me just what I missed ... I can thoroughly recommend this book to all those who are interested in motorcycle racing from 1946 to 1970, and those like me who thought they wouldn't be interested."
– *On The Level*

ISBN: 978-1-845847-93-7
Hardback • 22.5x15.2cm • £19.99* UK/$35.00* USA • 232 pages • 76 colour and b&w pictures

For more info on Veloce titles, visit our website at www.veloce.co.uk
• email: info@veloce.co.uk • Tel: +44(0)1305 260068
* prices subject to change, p&p extra

Index